CAMBRIDGE LIBRARY COLLECTION

Books of enduring scholarly value

History

The books reissued in this series include accounts of historical events and movements by eye-witnesses and contemporaries, as well as landmark studies that assembled significant source materials or developed new historiographical methods. The series includes work in social, political and military history on a wide range of periods and regions, giving modern scholars ready access to influential publications of the past.

A Short Historical Narrative of the Rise and Rapid Advancement of the Mahrattah State

James Kerr, a captain in the East India Company, translated this Persian text on the history of the Marathas in India. Published in 1782, it was one of the first English works to appear on the subject. Its content was compiled for Kerr by a Hindustani using Persian manuscripts and oral tradition. The Marathas had replaced the Mughal emperors as controllers of a large part of the sub-continent by the beginning of the eighteenth century, and it was inevitable that they would come into conflict with the East India Company. At the time of publication, the first of the three Anglo-Maratha wars had just ended, and interest in Indian affairs was great. Kerr denies any claim to be a historian, or to offer an analysis of his sources. The narrative outlines the growth of Maratha power from the seventeenth century, and concludes with a glossary of Indian terms.

Cambridge University Press has long been a pioneer in the reissuing of out-of-print titles from its own backlist, producing digital reprints of books that are still sought after by scholars and students but could not be reprinted economically using traditional technology. The Cambridge Library Collection extends this activity to a wider range of books which are still of importance to researchers and professionals, either for the source material they contain, or as landmarks in the history of their academic discipline.

Drawing from the world-renowned collections in the Cambridge University Library, and guided by the advice of experts in each subject area, Cambridge University Press is using state-of-the-art scanning machines in its own Printing House to capture the content of each book selected for inclusion. The files are processed to give a consistently clear, crisp image, and the books finished to the high quality standard for which the Press is recognised around the world. The latest print-on-demand technology ensures that the books will remain available indefinitely, and that orders for single or multiple copies can quickly be supplied.

The Cambridge Library Collection will bring back to life books of enduring scholarly value (including out-of-copyright works originally issued by other publishers) across a wide range of disciplines in the humanities and social sciences and in science and technology.

A Short Historical Narrative of the Rise and Rapid Advancement of the Mahrattah State

To the Present Strength and Consequence it has Acquired in the East

JAMES KERR

CAMBRIDGE
UNIVERSITY PRESS

CAMBRIDGE UNIVERSITY PRESS

Cambridge, New York, Melbourne, Madrid, Cape Town, Singapore,
São Paolo, Delhi, Dubai, Tokyo, Mexico City

Published in the United States of America by Cambridge University Press, New York

www.cambridge.org
Information on this title: www.cambridge.org/9781108027045

This edition first published 1782
This digitally printed version 2010

ISBN 978-1-108-02704-5 Paperback

A SHORT

HISTORICAL NARRATIVE

OF THE

MAHRATTAH STATE.

A SHORT

HISTORICAL NARRATIVE

OF

THE RISE AND RAPID ADVANCEMENT

OF THF

MAHRATTAH STATE,

TO THE PRESENT

STRENGTH AND CONSEQUENCE

IT HAS ACQUIRED IN THE EAST.

Written Originally in PERSIAN;
and tranflated into ENGLISH by

AN OFFICER IN THE EAST INDIA COMPANY'S SERVICE.

LONDON,
Printed by J. NICHOLS;
For T. CADELL, in the Strand.
MDCCLXXXII.

TO

LAURENCE SULLIVAN ESQUIRE

CHAIRMAN,

AND SIR WILLIAM JAMES BARONET

DEPUTY CHAIRMAN,

OF THE

COURT OF DIRECTORS

OF THE HON. UNITED

ENGLISH EAST INDIA COMPANY,

THIS

SHORT HISTORICAL NARRATIVE

IS

(WITH THEIR PERMISSION)

MOST RESPECTFULLY INSCRIBED

BY

THEIR MOST OBEDIENT

HUMBLE SERVANT,

JAMES KERR.

[v]

P R E F A C E.

THOUGH the Hindoo Government and Religion are known to have fubfifted all over India from the earlieft ages till the Mahometan invafions, and the Mahrattahs are only *one* of the various Tribes of the Hindoos; yet the power which is now underftood by the Mahrattah Empire, and which has been fo long formidable to others in the Eaft, does not feem to be of very ancient origin.

What compofes the following fheets is the fubftance of an account of its rife and progrefs given me above two years ago by a Mahometan native of Hindoftan, whom I retained

A   in

in my pay as a teacher of the Perfian Language. This man's knowledge and readinefs in the general
hiftory of his country induced me
to give more credit to his information than to any other I had opportunities of receiving; and my
opinion of him as a man of integrity,
intelligence, and obfervation, was the
more confirmed, from his having
been frequently felected as fuch by
fome gentlemen who had long refided in that part of the country, and
who like myfelf were anxious to have
with them an intelligent native, whofe
fituation and character in life gave
them confidence in his relation either
of the manners and cuftoms, or the
hiftorical events, of India.

It

It was at my particular defire that this man wrote the Narrative I now offer to the public, though at that time I had no idea in tranflating it beyond my own improvement in the language, and information on the fubject; otherwife it is probable the reader might have received likewife more information in perufing it than can now be well expected ; as in that cafe the plan no doubt would originally have been more extenfive, and the events compofing it more circumftantially related.

He had however my ftricteft injunctions to be careful in not mifleading me ; and under my own infpection he collected what he could

[viii]

from Perſian manuſcripts *. Oral tradition and the beſt received accounts
of the more recent times ſupplied the
reſt.

But, when the poſſibility ceaſes of
reputable authors and authentic re-
cords being conſulted, a narrative of
this kind cannot be expected to be
always very exact in the detail, either with regard to time, or the
leſs important circumſtances.

General notions are at moſt what
under ſuch diſadvantages it can convey; but even that is uſeful, eſpecially
as a general knowledge of this ſubject ſeems wanted, and as the hum-

* The only Hiſtorical Guide to this ſubject ;
ſince the Mahrattahs themſelves (as far as I
have been able to find out) have no ſuch of
their own,

ble

[ix]

ble attempt now made to communi-
cate that knowledge may lead and
induce to more minute refearches
others, whofe opportunities of information have been or may be more
favourable to fuccefs than fuch as I
I pretend to.

ɪ

Refpecting the tranflation, I fhall
only obferve, that though not a perfect
adept in the Perfian language, yet
my knowledge of the author's native
tongue * (the Moors) which a refidence

of

* The tranflation was principally made
when I had the immediate affiftance of the
writer of the original manufcript ; an advantage I carefully availed myfelf of, well knowing the neceffity in general of fuch a precaution ;
for, exclufive of every confideration refpecting
the language, there is but too frequently in
the native inhabitants (from whom the beft information might naturally be expected) a pre-
vailing fervility of fpirit, in wifhing at all events
6   to

of near ten years in India, not a
little application, and much intercourfe
with the natives, enabled me to acquire, fufficiently removed every in-
convenience arifing from deficiency in
that point.

Yet, after all, I own it is with dif-
fidence, and rather with reluctance,
that I publifh to the world what,
notwithftanding my own belief of the
facts, I never intended to have at
any rate gone farther than the fmall
circle of my intimates in India. But

to pleafe, with a diflike at the fame time to
betray their own ignorance ; which is a very
great bar to the fatisfaction of the European
enquirer, whofe aim is truth. Thofe gentlemen
who have refided any time in India, and made
the difpofition of the natives a part of their ftudy,
will, I believe, readily acknowledge the juftice
of this remark ; which my own experience and
repeated obfervation have long taught me to
guard againft.

the

the opinion of a few friends and refpectable characters in the literary world here has induced me to believe that, even fuppofing the imperfections it may not be altogether exempted from, fuch a narrative at this time would not be unacceptable or unterefting to the Public; and its being given folely for their information will, I truft, ferve much to fecure their candour for what errors in it they may now or hereafter difcover.

Before I conclude the preface, I deem it an act of juftice to the writer of the narrative (the original of which I have now before me) as well as for the fatisfaction of the reader, to remark, that the Hiftory of

the

the Mahometan Conquerors of Hindoftan, by Ferifhta, is quoted by
him as his authority for the firft
part of his account, viz. that of
Rhumba and Sumba. Another Perfian manufcript, which treats particularly of Allumgeer's [Aurungzebe]
conquefts, he fays, is his guide
concerning what refpeals the fecond
part, viz. that relative to Sewajie,
And the laft hiftorical record which
aided him in compiling this little
work I find to be the hiftory of
Bahadar Shaw, fon and fucceffor to
Aurungzebe.

JAMES KERR.

London,
Dec. 1, 1781.

A N

A N

HISTORICAL NARRATIVE, &c.

WE find by this Narrative that
what is now underſtood by
the Mahrattah State, had its origin but
about two hundred years ago : and
that Chance and Fortune have contributed more to its rapid riſe and pro-
greſs, than either the wiſdom of its
founder or the plans of his ſucceſ-
ſors.

It would perhaps be judged a pre-
ſumptuous prediction, and unauthoriz-
ed by appearances at this period, to ſay
that they have already arrived at their

B   higheſt

higheſt pitch of power; and that it would not be at all extraordinary if they are ſhortly ſeen loſing their influence in India, as quickly as we know they have acquired it. Yet it cannot be denied that however much their national character may favour the making of conqueſts, their political principles are not by any means calculated to preſerve them.

But this account of the Mahrattahs which I now give to the public, not touching upon their Civil Government, I ſhall not here intrude on the prerogative of an Hiſtorian, but confine myſelf intirely to that of a Tranſlator, and in idiom only ſhall I differ from the original, which ſimply relates ſuch hiſtorical events and military tranſactions, as have had an evident

dent tendency in aggrandizing a people, who, from what we can learn, till the æra abovementioned, has only been known, even in their own country, as one of the various cafts, or tribes of that religion, which, from the moft ancient hiftory, appears to have been the eftablifhed one in Hindoftan.

The firft Mahrattah Chief who fettled at Sattarah (the chief feat of the ftill nominal fovereign of thefe people) was one Rhumba, a native of Oodapoor, the capital of Marawar. He was not then called Rajah, but only Chief, or Rowfaib. Twenty cofs round that place, terminated the bounds of his government. He had a body of betwixt two and three thoufand horfe, confifting rather of

thofe

thofe who chofe to follow and fhare his fortune, than troops in regular pay. With thefe he ufed to ravage and plunder the neighbouring countries of the Cockun Ahmudnagur, and Bejapoor; and by fuch means, more than by the revenue of his own uncultivated diftrict, he collected about three lack of rupees a year. His perfonal retinue confifted of about 100 good horfe, an elephant, and fome camels. It was he who firft built the fort of Sattarah, which has fince been encreafed from time to time. His father was coufin to the Oodapoor Rajah; and though a man or no particular confequence in the government, yet, from his connection with the Rajah, he had a ftated falary for the fupport of his family.

Rhumba

Rhumba was a youth of diſſipated manners : and one day, ſoon after his father's death, when he was in a ſtate of intoxication, he murdered a man ; for which crime he was immediately confined; and notwithſtanding all the intereſt that could be made for him, the Rajah was determined on putting him to death ; but his mother bribed the gaoler to permit his eſcape. This malconduct of his was the original cauſe of that mode of life to which he afterwards betook himſelf, and which indeed ſeems to have been beſt adapted to his roving ſpirit. He fled to Eugene, the capital of Malwa; and from thence, after a few days ſtay, he proceeded to Aſſeer, in the province of Kandeſs ; and there he entered

B 3   into

into the fervice of Rajah Alee Kawn.
Diftinguifhing himfelf on fome occafion in the character of a private
feapoy, he was promoted to the command of an hundred horfe, in which
ftation he gained both credit and
wealth. He remained at Affeer till
the death of his benefactor, who
leaving no iffue, that province fell
under the dominion of the king of
Delli, then Jehanguire, on which
Rhumba had his fortune again to feek.

It was at this time he went and
fettled at Sattarah, where he lived, in
the manner as related, forty years.

Rhumba was fucceeded by his only
fon Sumba; who, in imitation of his
father, lived by maroding the neighbouring countries; and this he was
the better enabled to do, by the riches
which

which had defcended to him. He awed the whole Decan, and obliged many of its Zemindars to pay him a chout or tribute, by confenting to which they were freed from his pillaging excurfions.

By thefe means his annual income amounted to fix lack of rupees, which enabled him to keep up a body of five thoufand horfe. He, and Jacoot Cawn Hubfhie, a governor of Rajpoorie, were in the ftricteft friendfhip, and, acting in concert, ufed frequently to enjoy the fruits of their rapine together. Sumba latterly poffeffed great wealth, from the following caufe.

Mullick Umber Hubfhie, governor of Dowlatabad, having thrown off his allegiance to the king of Bejapoor, to

B 4   whom

whom he was a tributary, and de-
pending on the ſtrength of his fort,
and the flouriſhing ſtate of his treaſury, he for ſome years omitted paying the uſual tribute to that prince,
who at laſt ſent an army to bring him
to ſubjection.

Mullick Umber, upon this occaſion, applied to Sumba for his aid;
and that chief, ſeeing the proſpect of
advantage, which would accrue to him
from his compliance, loſt no time in
repairing to Dowlatabad, with his
whole force, and by his aſſiſtance,
Mullick Umber gained a compleat
victory over his maſter's troops; which
being reported to the Bejapoor king,
he wrote privately to Sumba, upbraiding him for having engaged as an ally
with

with a flave*, and at the fame time inviting him to join in the caufe of juftice, and affift in punifhing the rebel, promifing to reward him with half the treafure that might be found in Dowlatabad. To which Sumba replied, that if he (the king) would make over to him the right of a certain portion of land (which he defcribed) either from Bejapoor or Dowlatabad, he would in that cafe take upon himfelf the reduction of Mullick Umber to obedience.

The king, unwilling to give up the entire right to any part of his dominions, would not accede to this

* Mullick Umber had been originally a flave of Nizam Beyhrie's, the former governor of Dowlatabad, who had adopted him as his own, and thereby fucceeded to his fortunes ; a thing not extraordinary in the Eaft.

pro-

propoſal, but, as an equivalent for
what ſervices Sumba might perform,
promiſed him a chout from his whole
revenue. Sumba judged this offer
too advantageous to be rejected ; and
the alliance he had formed with Umber was not, according to his ideas, a
ſufficient cauſe for his not accepting
it. How the buſineſs was to be ac-
compliſhed was his only concern. He
wrote to the Buckſhie of the king's
troops, who, upon his defeat, had re-
treated with his army near the capital,
Bejapoor; that, in order more eaſily
to effect the purpoſe, it would be requiſite ſtill to preſerve an appearance
of friendſhip with Umber, and therefore he propoſed remaining at Dowlatabad, till the Buckſhie ſhould approach with his troops, which he
urged

urged the neceſſity of doing with all
poſſible ſpeed; for he dreaded that a
delay might diſcover his treachery,
and thereby render his ſervices un-
neceſſary to either party, and moſt
likely inſure the reſentment of one of
them.

The Buckſhie, on the receipt of
Sumba's letter, marched with all poſſible ſpeed to Dowlatabad, where, on
his near approach, he found that
Umber, with his ſuppoſed friend
Sumba, was encamped. Hoſtilities
ſoon commenced, and ſkirmiſhes continued, for five or ſix days, without
any ſuperiority gained on either ſide.
Sumba, who had not yet thrown off
the maſk, during this time was rather
a ſpectator, than an actor in the field,
except in preparing for the execution

I   of

of his fcheme, by giving frequent intelligence to the Buckfhie of all Umber's plans, which he was well-ena-
bled to do, by the confidence which
that unfortunate man repofed in him.

After fome days had thus elapfed,
he withdrew his party to a fmall diftance from Umber, to whom (in order to prevent fufpicion) he went in
perfon, and accounted for this ma-
nœuvre, by propofing, as the moft eli-
gible method to infure victory, that
he would ftand aloof, as a corps of
referve, to fupport him as neceffity
might require. This was readily
agreed to by the unwary Umber.
Towards noon, Sumba fent to acquaint
the Buckfhie, that now was the time
for deciding who fhould be conquer-
or, defiring he would immediately

com-

commence an attack; and that he (Sumba) would at the fame time, di-rect his, on a different quarter.

Having previoufly affembled his officers, and given orders, that his people fhould put no balls in their pieces; but only to preferve the ap-pearance of oppofing the Buckfhie's troops, till he fhould give the fignal to draw their fabres, when they were in-ftantly to ufe them againft thofe of Umber. He now advanced, as if to fupport the man, whofe ruin he was meditating, and at laft effected.

Umber, who little fufpected the perfidious plot of his profeft friend, and having likewife the utmoft con-fidence in his courage and military fkill, was eafily prevailed upon by him to retire, with a few attendants,

to

to refresh himself under the shade of
some trees on the banks of an adjacent tank ; for by this time he had
sustained some of the enemy's onsets,
and had attacked likewise in his turn.
Sumba soon gave the signal to his
troops ; and when Umber's son, who
remained in the field, discovered the
treachery, he sent immediately to
acquaint his father therewith, and determined to sell his own life as dear
as possible. But after dealing destruc-
tion to many of those who pressed on
him, he was at last slain, being overpowered by numbers, before he could
receive any assistance from Umber,
who, when preparing to come to his
son's relief, was surrounded by a party
from the Buckshie's army ; and though
he made every effort that courage and
despair

defpair could fuggeft, yet at laft, being covered with wounds, faint with fatigue, the lofs of blood, and want of water, he fell down, and was carried to the Buckfhie's tent, where he foon after died. A total rout of his army enfued,

After Umber's defeat in the field, the Buckfhie and his friend Sumba went towards the fort of Dowlatabad, which was now in an entire defencelefs ftate. Umber's wife, however, could not be prevailed on to open the gates, till fhe was fatisfied that herfelf, with the other women of her family, would be permitted to go where they pleafed, without the leaft violence being offered to their honour. This the Buckfhie agreed to, but would not permit their carrying any thing off,

off, except their wearing apparel ; at the fame time affuring them, in that cafe, of an efcort to conduct them, in fafety, to wherever they chofe to go. Matters being thus adjufted, the third day after the battle, the Buckfhie took poffeffion of the fort, and fent the women of Umber's houfe to the Rajpoorie governor, through whom Umber's unfortunate acquaintance with Sumba firft commenced.

When thefe tidings reached the Bejapoor king, he was elated with joy, and, being defirous to vifit the city and caftle of Dowlatabad, he fet out, and foon arrived at that place, where finding immenfe wealth, he paid Sumba much more than the price agreed on for his treachery, and after treating him with many marks of dif-
tinction,

tinction, he conferred on him the title of Rajah, and gave him the grants for the chouts, as before ſtipulated.

Sumba was the firſt Rajah (according to this account) that ever was in Sattarah, which in his time only began to be populous. When he was ſo promoted, he forſook his original way of life, that of maroding and plundering, and lived in a manner more becoming his new dignity. He uſed after this period to pay a viſit regularly twice a year to his benefactor the Bejapoor king, who always ſhewed him great reſpect; at one time in particular, when the king's ſon was married, Sumba with his whole family went by invitation to celebrate the nuptials.

C

When

When the king died, his eldeſt ſon
and ſucceſſor Abrahim Adil Shaw
ſhewed Sumba the ſame marks of
friendſhip and attention as his father
had aone, and uſed to employ him
whenever he had occaſion for his
military ſkill and prowefs, having
great reliance on him, as a man
poſſeſſed, in an ample degree, of
both. Sumba, when he was ninety
years of age, and of courſe unfit to
undergo the fatigues of campaign-
ing, delivered over the command of
his troops to his only ſon Sewajie,
then about thirty years old, and ſent
him to Bejapoor, to perform what
ſervices the young king might require
of him. Sumba but a ſhort while
ſurvived his retirement ; and was
ſucceeded by the above mentioned
Sewajie, who, ſoon after his father's

death,

death, was confirmed in the title of
Rajah by the Bejapoor king, in a
full Mujlifs, or court, affembled for
that purpofe.

Sumba by his own abilities and
courage, with an unremitted exertion
of cunning and fineffe, the true cha-
racteriftics of a Mahrattah, had raifed
himfelf by a rapid progrefs to that
degree of confequence we fee him
arrived at; and Sattarah was now
become of confiderable importance
from the tributes annexed to it.

It was about this time Shaw Jehan
fent his fon Aurungzebe to fubdue
the young king of Bejapoor, Abra-
ham Adil Shaw; who, after his father's death, had thrown off his allegiance to the court of Dehli; and
that city being reduced by the death

of

of the king, who fell in battle, Sewajie fled to his own capital of Sattarah;
but Aurungzebe forefeeing that the
turbulent and ambitious fpirit of that
chief would ever be dangerous to
the peace of the decan, fent a de-
tachment to lay Sattarah wafte, and
if poffible to get hold of Sewajie
himfelf; but, on the approach of his
purfuers, Sewajie made his efcape to
Gueriah. Sattarah on this occafion
was plundered and burnt, but no
force left behind, as the country
round was thought of but little confequence.

Sewajie, after remaining a twelvemonth at Gueriah, feeing no prof-
pect of Aurungzebe's quitting the
decan, turned his thoughts towards
getting firmly fettled in his own
dominions;

dominions; and for this purpofe he went, in an humble manner, with his family, to Bejapoor, and wrote a petition, which was prefented to Aurungzebe, and feconded by that prince's Dewan, who was a Hindoo, and well inclined to Sewajie's inter‑efts; fetting forth, that both he and his father were Zemindars, or land‑holders of the Bejapoor king, and by the tenor of their grants were obliged to attend whenever his fer‑vice required it, but now that the decan was fubdued, and in poffeffion of the king of Dehli, he hoped that he might be forgiven for what had paf‑fed, and permitted to take poffeffion of his former teritories, with the chout confirmed to him, as in the king of Bejapoor's time; for all which he would

C 3   be

be ready to execute what fervices he might be ordered to perform. Aurungzebe was prevailed on, though with reluctance, to reſtore and confirm Sewajie in Sattarah; but as to the chout he petitioned for, his father's, Shaw Jehan, permiſſion was firſt to be obtained.

Sewajie, upon this anfwer, only in part fatisfactory, was ſtill importunate with his requeſt, that Aurungzebe, whom he looked upon, he faid, as his benefactor and protector, would intercede with his father for the confirmation of the chout, as it was impoſſible for him to go to Dehli, or otherwife gain his point, but through his interceſſion. The prince however gave him to underſtand, that till he had rendered him fome piece of fervice, and fhewn himfelf

worthy

worthy of favour, he need expect
no further indulgence than had
been already granted him. And
Sewajie, finding the prince determined, loft no further time, but
went to Sattarah, and remained quiet
during the five following years, without enjoying the chout he wifhed
for, or attempting by force to make
good his pretenfions.

When Aurungzebe, by his father's
orders, left that part of the country,
to enforce the payment of a tribute
from Tanna Shaw, the king of the
province of Telingan (whofe capital
is Hyderabad), he then found it ne-
ceffary to put Sewagie's abilities and
attachment to the teft, as Tanna Shaw
refufed to comply with the demands
that were made of him, alledging,

C 4   that

that his forefathers, who had fat on that throne during a great length of time, had never paid the tribute required by the king of Dehli; and at the fame time avowed himfelf ready to refift force by force, fhould any be ufed to compel obedience. The rainy feafon now approaching, Aurungzebe declined commencing hoftilities himfelf, as he could not ftay to profecute the fiege ; he therefore refolved to employ Sewajie to lay wafte the country, which, from his knowledge of it, and the Mahrattah mode of fighting, he was well calculated to effect. Sewajie was accordingly fent for; and the prince told him, that if he would remain near Hyderabad, and by maroding, pillaging, and otherwife deftroying the country, weaken the power of Tanna Shaw, he would fe-

cure

cure to him the chout he formerly
petitioned for. Having given Sewajie
fome money for the payment of his
troops, and recommended to him to
avoid rifking a general engagement
with what force Tanna Shaw might
fend to oppofe him, Aurungzebe returned to Bejapoor.

Sewajie, in compliance with the
prince's commands, continued on the
borders of Hyderabad for near a year,
executing the orders he had received;
when at laft Tanna Shaw, tired out
with the inroads of an enemy he never
could fubdue, and in order to preferve
his diftreffed diftricts from entire ruin,
wrote to Sewajie, upbraiding him for
entering into the fervice of the king
of Dehli, and thus deftroying that
country which had given them both
birth,

birth, meaning the Decan; and at the fame time offering him a chout from his revenues, if he would defift from his depredations, and form an alliance with him.

Sewajie was well pleafed with this propofal; but fearing the wrath of Aurungzebe, he was obliged to act cautioufly. He wrote, in anfwer to Tanna Shaw, that fince the king of Dehli had got poffeffion of Bejapoor, his power and authority were great in the Decan; and that neceffity alone had obliged him to acknowledge the conqueror, who had agreed to reftore his chout for the fervices he was now employed upon. But if Tanna Shaw would make over to him a chout from his province, he would leave off molefting him, and form a friendfhip

with

with him ; only, that the bufinefs
muft be managed with addrefs, left
it fhould come to the ears of Aurungzebe.

Sewajie, on receiving the requifite
grants from Tanna Shaw, adopted
the moft likely method to promote
his own views, and to preferve the
fecrecy fo favourable to their fuccefs.
He wrote to Aurungzebe; fetting
forth the fervices he had performed,
which, he faid, no doubt, muft have
been related to him by the diftreffed
people of the country he had laid
wafte; and, pretending a bad ftate of
health, he requefted leave to return
to Sattarah. This Aurungzebe confented to ; but infifted that he fhould
leave behind him fome trufty troops,
who were well acquainted with the
country,

country, in order to continue the de-
ſtructive depredations he had begun.

Sewajie accordingly came to Sattarah, but brought with him the flower
of his army. The few he left behind
were only to preſerve appearances.

Much about this time Shaw Jehan's affairs towards Cabul and Kan-
dehaar required the preſence of Aurungzebe and his army, who, in conſequence of orders from Dehli, left
Bejapoor with only a ſmall body of
troops for its ſafety, and the peace of
the Decan. Tanna Shaw thought this
a favourable opportunity to retaliate
for the injuries he had ſuffered; and
accordingly ſet out for Bejapoor; and
ſent for Sewajie, who, ſecretly repin-
ing that his chout had been ſtopt
ever ſince Aurungzebe had got poſ-
feffion

feffion of that country, and thinking this an excellent opportunity to fecure himfelf, without waiting the fulfilment of Aurungzebe's promifes, readily came to Tanna Shaw's affiftance, in order to compleat his engagement.

The Naib, whom Aurungzebe left behind him, falling in battle, his whole troops were beat off the field. The Killidar of the fort then fent to Sewajie, to expoftulate with him for fo ungrateful a conduct to his benefactor, and thus repaying the lenity and favour that had been fhewn him on a former occafion, when Bejapoor was fubdued by Aurungzebe, at which time he had fled from that place, and likewife from his own fort (Sattarah); but, by the indulgence of the conqueror, he had been permitted to

7   return

return and enjoy in peace the laft-
mentioned place : that his now taking the advantage of Aurungzebe's
abfence to be acceffary in bringing
and affifting his enemies, was treachery and ingratitude of the deepeft
dye. Sewajie denied the charge of
having brought Tannah Shaw againft
Bejapoor ; and faid, that he had only
joined him from a motive of recovering what was his right, fince Aurungzebe had refufed paying him the
chout the former king of Bejapoor
had done. But if he (the Killidar)
would confent to pay him the arrears
on that fcore, he would engage to
remove Tannah Shaw's army. The
Killidar, knowing the place muft fall
if the enemy perfifted, agreed to pay
him feven lack of rupees. Sewajie

6   how-

however fent to inform him that that
was not fufficient ; for that Tannah
Shaw would not be prevailed upon to
withdraw his army without a fum
equivalent to the expence he had
been at. To which the Killidar replied, that he would confent to a fmall
amount ; but had it not in his power
to give any thing confiderable.

Sewajie, thinking the fuccefs of
the fiege precarious, and having no
reafon to be diffatisfied with the terms
he had made for himfelf, and not
entirely free from the apprehenfion
of the confequence that might enfue
on Aurungzebe's being informed of
his behaviour, ftrongly advifed Tannah Shaw, with whom he had much
influence, to accept of fome money,
and relinquifh the attempt of taking
the

the place, fince it would coft him much ; and the fuccefs was far from being certain, as the fort was ftrong, and he had reafon to believe was well provided for a defence. He likewife urged, that if Aurungzebe fhould return, and oblige them to raife the fiege, it would be difgraceful to both. So having fecured feven lack of rupees for himfelf, and feven lack for Tannah Shaw, Bejapoor was imme-diately freed from any fears from that quarter, by Tannah Shaw and his ally Sewajie withdrawing their troops to Hyderabad.

One year's chout foon became due from Tannah Shaw to Sewajie ; it was paid without hefitation, notwithftand-ing he had of his own free will given Sewajie the feven lack of rupees he

had

had received from Bejapoor, befides many other valuable prefents. The neceffity Tannah Shaw perceived to keep Sewajie firm in his intereft, accounts for his apparent liberality. Sewajie, having thus increafed his wealth, returned to Sattarah.

When Shaw Jehawn was informed of Tannah Shaw's expedition; and of his being affifted by Sewajie againft Bejapoor, he confulted with Saddula Cawn, his prime minifter, about fending an expedition to extirpate both Tannah Shaw and Sewajie from the Decan. The vizier however advifed him to poftpone the expedition till Aurungzebe fhould return from the northward, as, by his having been already in that country, he was the

fitteft

fitteft man to be employed on the
propofed fervice.

Aurungzebe, on his return to
Dhelli, was accordingly fent to the
Decan, but he was prevented from
profecuting the fcheme of punifhing
the difturbers of the empire in that
quarter by a quarrel with his eldeft
brother, Darafhikoo ; who, jealous
of the power and reputation which
that prince was acquiring by his expeditions, prevailed upon his father
to recall Aurungzebe from the Decan,
and agree to fend his own fon, So-
lomon Shikoo, a youth about twenty-
two years of age, to execute this
undertaking. The order for Aurungzebe's return, which Shaw Jehawn granted with fo much reluctance, forefeeing the bad confequence

that

that would attend this meafure, reached him when he had advanced as far
as the Malwa Province. He was preparing to obey his father's fummons,
when he had intelligence from court
what were the motives of this fudden
alteration, and who was to fucceed
him, to put in execution the fervice it
was firft intended he fhould perform.
He thereupon wrote to his father, re-
prefenting as a grievance his being
recalled without any fufficient reafon
being affigned; and that another
being fent to execute the fame duty,
implied his inability to the tafk. He
therefore declined returning; and
waited where he was, for further in-
ftructions.

When Shaw Jehawn received Aurungzebe's letter, he fhewed it to Da-

rafhikoo;

raſhikoo ; telling him, with concern,
that he now perceived the conſe-
quences beginning, which he had fore-
told, and warned him againſt. Daraſhikoo immediately propoſed going
in perſon, with a force ſufficient to
enſure his brother's obedience to the
royal mandate. The king, though
entirely averſe to this ſcheme, was ſo
wrapt up in his favourite ſon, that he
had not reſolution enough to put a
negative on any thing he propoſed,
however abſurd. Daraſhikoo accordingly ſet out, and came up with his
brother near Eugene (the Malwa capital), where a battle enſued, in
which Daraſhikoo met with an entire
defeat, and ſaved himſelf by flight.
His whole encampment fell into the
hands of Aurungzebe, who ſoon

after

after this fuccefs purfued his march towards Ackburabad, in order to prevent Darafhikoo getting into power again. On his near approach to the capital, he wrote to his friends * at court, and requefted them to intercede with his father, at the fame time making proteftations of his readinefs to o-bey whatfoever orders he might receive, either to proceed to the Decan, or attend the king, who, though almoft inconfolable for what had paffed, yet, in order to prevent an increafe of the evils with which the complexion of the times was fo replete, confented to Aurungzebe's return. Soon he had too fatal proofs of that prince's intrigues.

* Amongft whom, and not of the leaft ufe to him, was one of his fifters, who had warmly entered into all his views. Shaw Jehawn had two daughters, who took oppofite parties in their brothers' contentions.

Shaw

Shaw Jehawn's own imprifonment
firft, and then that of his favourite
fon, whom he wifhed to have fucceeded him, were the ultimate fteps
by which Aurungzebe afcended the
throne.

It is to be obferved, that when
Aurungzebe heard of his brother
coming againft him, he wrote to another brother of his, Muradbukfh, then
governor of the Guzerat province,
to come to his affiftance; who, from
Aurungzebe's reprefentation of the
elder brother's conduct, and affurances
of the benefit he would reap by oppofing him, readily confented to his
requeft, and joined him accordingly,
before Darafhikoo came up. Darafhikoo, upon his defeat, went to
Dhelli, where having fupplied him

felf

felf with fome treafure, he fled to Lahore *.

Sewajie, taking advantage of the domeftic diffentions in Shaw Jehawn's family, which at this time fubfifted through every branch of it (and thereby greatly weakened the power and influence of the government), af-fembled all the force he could, in or-der to attack fuch places of the Decan as acknowledged the king of Dhelli; and though he could not reduce the

* In this, as well as in other parts of the nrrrative which treat particularly of the Mo-gul hiftory, I am fenfible it differs often, and fometimes materially, from the Englifh writers on the fubjeɛt; and though I fhould never pre-fume, but on the cleareft conviɛtion, to call in queftion what is related by refpeɛtable hifto-rians, yet I could not condefcend to deviate from the original merely to make it tally with other accounts, unlefs I was firft convinced that my own author (if I may ufe the expref-fion) was particularly to be doubted.

forts

forts of Barampoor, Aurungzabad, Dawlatabad, Ahmudnegur, Bejapoor, and Bedur; yet, after laying wafte and deftroying the villages of thofe diftricts, the diftreffed inhabitants, finding they could expect no relief from their own capitals, were under the neceffity of fubmitting; and a-greed to pay the revenue to him. The governors of thefe places did not fail to give intelligence to the court of Dhelli of what was going on. But the diftracted ftate of that empire would not then admit of fending a force to fuch a diftance, fufficient to punifh the refractory Mahrattah, who, in the courfe of three years, from the commencement of Aurungzebe's quarrels with his brother, laid almoft the whole Decan under his fubjection. The forts

of

of Poorunder, Logur, Naffick, Tre-
muck, Jalnapoor, Galna, Dabul,
Culliany, Rhimrie, Kurnalla, Purna-
la, Cheul, Hunkie, Tunkie, Mudgur,
Hudgur, with many other fmall forts,
yielded to the conqueror; thofe in the
Cockin near the fea-coaft belonged to
Jacoot Cawn Hubfhie, governor of
Rajpoorie, with whom Sewajie was in
friendfhip, and were therefore permitted to remain unmolefted.

Shaw Jehawn being dead, and Aurungzebe, who fucceeded his father,
having now nothing to fear from the
infurrections of his brothers (one of
them having been cut off, and the
other two in his poffeffion), and having reigned undifturbed in every other
part of his dominions except the Decan,
for upwards of ten years, he turned
his

his attention to the fettling of that quarter from whence he had fo many complaints of Sewajie, and determined to extirpate from it thofe who had taken the advantage of his abfence to throw off their allegiance. After having allotted to his fons, and the different Oomrahs, their feveral trufts, he fet out to purfue his fcheme of fubduing his rebellious fubjects in the Decan.

Tannah Shaw and Sewajie were the two who had principally incurred his difpleafure; the latter in particular had raifed himfelf to an aftonifhing degree of power, by his depredations in the different parts of that country, of which in fact he was become entirely mafter, and to punifh him was Aurungzebe's firft defign. He ac-

cordingly

cordingly came to Sattarah with a large
army.

Sewajie, who to a deep under-
ftanding added an extraordinary fhare
of perfonal courage, was not to be in-
timidated by the appearance only of
an army fo much fuperior to his own;
but with his body of near thirty
thoufand men (which he had then in
his fervice), he hefitated not to face
the enemy. Senfible however of his
own inferiority, he wifely avoided
coming to any general engagement,
but in the Mahrattah way continually
kept harraffing the king's troops, by
beating up their quarters in the night,
and attacking their foraging parties:
neither did he neglect the method of
poifoning the neighbouring tanks and
wells, from which the enemy were to
have

have their water, by throwing into them the toor or milkbufh*.

During fix months the two armies lay near each other, though nothing decifive was produced, yet feveral forts, which had been reduced by Sewajie, were again falling into the poffeffion of Aurungzebe's officers, many of whom had been detached properly provided to effect that pur-pofe, while he himfelf remained near Sattarah.

* When obliged to retreat before a fuperior force, or in laying wafte the country in the neighbourhood of an enemy's encampment, it is cuftomary with Eaftern armies, particularly Mahrattah ones, to throw into tanks and wells, from which the enemy is fupplied with water, this fpecies of fhrub, from which, when broken or bruifed, there iffues a poifonous milky juice, whereby thefe refervoirs are rendered ufelefs, till the return of the rainy feafon, when the wells are cleanfed out, and the tanks, being dried up, are fit to receive the water as it falls.

Au-

Aurungzebe wifhed much to bring Sewajie to action. He fent a meffage to him, upbraiding him for his daftardly manner of fighting, and telling him, that it did not become one, who affumed to himfelf the name of a valiant warrior, to adopt a method ufed only by thieves and maroders; but that, like a brave foldier, he ought to meet his enemy face to face. This, however, had not the defired effect: Sewajie's reply was, that he was a Mahrattah, and fought in the manner practifed by thofe people. In the courfe of a twelvemonth, however, from the time Aurungzebe came into the Decan, though he could not intirely fubdue Sewajie, yet moft of the country acknowledged his authority; and for what he could not effect by force, he had recourfe to ftratagem.

2   Sewajie

Sewajie being now deprived of the revenues of the country, and the other refources which enabled him to fupport his army; Aurungzebe naturally concluded, that it would not be a difficult matter to get over to his fide feveral of Sewajie's principal officers, which he attempted with fuccefs, by promifing Jaghires, and other rewards. This fcheme being planned, and Jaifing, the Rajah of Janagur, a chief of the Hindoo religion in Aurungzebe's army, being fecurity to the leaders of thofe of Sewajie's troops, who were coming over to the king's party, it was put in execution in the following manner.

Jaderow, at the head of Sewajie's malcontents, went, with feveral other officers, to Sewajie, and pro-

pofed

[47]

pofed to him, to go with their people, and attack the enemy; which he readily agreed to, and faid, he himfelf would follow and fupport them. Jaderow had previoufly fent, to let Aurungzebe know that they were that day coming to join him. The king, that thefe chiefs might put the more confidence in him, fent the Rajah Jaifing, his negociator, to meet them; and, on their coming into the camp, he ordered them to be faluted with a general difcharge of his cannon; which Sewajie hearing, imagined the troops were engaged, and inftantly haftened to their affiftance. But on his nearer approach to the king's camp, he was aftonifhed to fee nothing of his advanced party; and much enraged when he difcovered

I   their

their treachery *. This however did not difpirit him ; he fent to know the caufe of their difguft, and why they had thus deferted him. To which they gave for anfwer, that they were convinced he muft at laft fall a victim to his own obftinacy ; as Aurungzebe, who was acknowledged and obeyed by the whole Decan, would not defift from his enterprize till it was compleated by his fall ; nor did they think it advifeable to involve themfelves in his ruin. This reply enraged him more than ever, and with the remainder of his army, now not exceeding ten or twelve thoufand men, he furioufly charged the king's

* Some conferences had previoufly taken place betwixt Sewajie and thefe chiefs, relative to arrears of pay, and his profpects of holding his ground ; but the entire repulfe of Aurungzebe from the Decan was the only thing he could be prevailed on to liften to,

troops,

troops, and feveral on both fides fell
in the onfet. The party, confifting
of ten thoufand men, who deferted
him, were at this time drawn up at
a little diftance from the main body of
the king's troops; and on Sewajie's re-
tiring from the firft charge they prevented his retreat, and attacked him on
another quarter. A general and moft
bloody action enfued, in which fome
thoufands fell on each fide. Many of
Sewajie's people, whofe hearts failed
them, threw down their arms, and
attempted to fave themfelves by flight;
the more valiant of them continued
fighting or bravely dying by his
fide. He himfelf was at laft left
with only a few; and though his
horfe was wounded under him, he
continued fighting on foot, and dif-

E   playing

playing aftonifhing acts of valour and
defpair. Some of Aurungzebe's officers, who had by this time clofely
furrounded him, told him, that, if
he wifhed for his own prefervation,
he would lay down his fword, and
fubmit to be carried in fafety to the
king, who had given particular directions not to wound him, if poffible. To which he replied, that it
did not become a man, and an officer, to lay down his arms; nor
would he (he faid) while he had life
left in his body, part with his fword
from his hand. By this time Aurungzebe came up himfelf, where
Sewajie fat almoft exhaufted, and
addreffed him, by telling him, that
he was an eye-witnefs of his valour,
of which there could remain no doubt;

but

but it was in vain for him fingly to
oppofe his fate againft fuch numbers; and affured him, at the fame
time, of refpectful treatment, if he
would lay down his fword, and
yield to the fortune which it was
impoffible for him now to evade.
Sewajie, overcome by fatigue and
thirft, and feeing the folly of
further refiftance, at laft yielded
to the conqueror; but not without
faying, that the want of bodily
ftrength only had prevailed upon him
to furrender; for that, if he could
have been refrefhed by a little water,
he would have given him ftill greater proofs of his fpirit.

By the capture of Sewajie, Sattarah fell into the hands of Aurung-

zebe, about the year of the Hijera one thoufand one hundred and two.

Sewajie, who with his whole family became Aurungzebe's prifoners, at this time had only one fon remaining, a youth of about twelve or thirteen years of age, the fame who has fince been known by the name of Sowrajah. An elder fon died about the time that Rajah engaged in the fervice of Aurungzebe, in his firft expedition into the Decan againft Bejapoor.

About a year after this cataftrophe of Sewajie's affairs, a fifter of his, by name Tarabahie, by the means of Affud Kawn, gained admittance to the prince's prefence, and in a fupplicant manner petitioned for the releafe of herfelf, Sewajie's fon, and

the

[53]

the women of the family ; whofe only crime was, their connection with Sewajie. She begged likewife, that they might be reftored to their family refidence of Sattarah. This requeft fhe enforced by prefenting Sewajie's fon, whofe confinement was ill adapted to his weakly conftitution, and had much increafed an illnefs he laboured under.

The king was moved with compaffion, and fo far complied with the old lady's requeft, as to give them their liberty ; but would not confent to their refiding at Sattarah. Sewajie now only remained a prifoner; the reft of his family, accompanied by Bejerow, went to Nagpoor, the capital of Berar.

E 3   When

When Sewajie had been about three
years a prifoner, and was defpairing
of ever getting his liberty from Aurungzebe, he had recourfe to ftratagem to obtain it. He pretended that,
when his fon was fick, he had made
a vow to beftow on his recovery a certain fum in acts of charity and bene-
volence; that now, having accounts
of his fon's health being reftored, he
wifhed to difcharge his vow; and he
meant, by the king's permiffion, to
let his army fhare in his generofity.

This indulgence was readily granted; and for fix days confections *

were

* The giving confectionaries to foldiers may
no doubt appear ftrange; but, as every country
has cuftoms peculiar to itfelf, fo in the Eaft,
where the ufe of fpirits is not admitted, the foldiery in the armies, on birth-days or other extraordinary occafions, have fweetmeats, tobacco,
and opium, according to the cafts who are to
par-

were carrying out of his tent for the
foldiers; on the feventh day, watching
an opportunity about noon, when
there were few attendants near him,
he fhut himfelf up in one of the baf-
kets, and was carried out by a faithful domeftic paft his unfufpecting
guards to the tent of the king's dewan,
who was a Hindoo, and with whom
Sewajie had previoufly concerted meafures for his efcape : he was kept
here till the evening, when, putting on
the tattered garb of an Halkara, he
made the beft of his way about five
cofs diftant from the camp, where he
mounted a horfe which was ready for

partake, ferved out to them, as the Englifh
give drams or punch. This attention to the
Company's native troops is prudently alfo very
often obferved, as the officer who commands
may fee it advifeable, to prevent the baneful
feeds of jealoufy and difcontent.

E 4   him,

him, and travelled that night thirty cofs. In a few days he arrived at Nagpoor. Not thinking himfelf fafe here, he went to Gueriah, where he lived concealed for two years, notwithftanding all the fearch that was made for him by order of Aurungzebe; but at laft grief and vexation for his misfortunes, and defpair of ever being able to remove them, brought on an illnefs, of which he foon died.

The news of Sewajie's death reached the king about four months after. This happened about the fame time that his wife wrote to Jaderow, and the other chiefs who had deferted Sewajie when Aurungzebe lay before Sattarah, expoftulating with them, by the misfortunes which their ungrateful

grateful conduct brought upon Sewajie and his family, by joining the
enemy in the day of his diftrefs ; and
as they had eftablifhed their fortunes by
his ruin; that it behoved them, being
men of the fame caft, (now Sewajie was
dead) to recompence, as far was poffible, their want of fidelity to him,
by doing juftice to his fon and family,
and endeavouring to procure to them
Sattarah as a place of refidence ; they
at that time experiencing the greateft
adverfity, and even fubfifting by the
charity of their friends.

Jaderow, on receipt of this letter, affembled the Mahrattah chiefs,
when it was agreed by them to prefent to the king a petition in behalf of Sewajie's family, and to ac-
company it with the widow's letter

to

to Jaderow. Aurungzebe was prevailed upon to acquiefce fo far as
to permit the family's going to live
at Sattarah (the young Rajah only ex-
cepted, who fhould attend his army
till he might have an opportunity
of fhewing himfelf worthy of favour).
The Souraja accordingly attended Aurungzebe (not as a prifoner, but) at
the head of fome of his father's adherents. His mother, with the reft
of his family, went to Sattarah.

In the courfe of two years the Souraja acquitted himfelf, on feveral occafions, as an active and brave officer,
and much to the fatisfaction of Aurungzebe, who beftowed on him feveral marks of honour, and gave
him the proper writs to take Sattarah
and the original diftricts belonging to
it; making him, however, give an
obli-

obligation under his hand, that he would obey the king's fummons whenever he fhould be called upon.

The Souraja remained quiet at Sattarah during the life of Aurungzebe, being apprehenfive of incurring the difpleafure of that prince, who ftill remained about the Decan, after having entirely fubdued that country *, till

* Though the Mogul empire was more extenfive in Aurungzebe's reign than in that of any of the preceding Emperors ; yet it is certainly paying him too great a compliment to fay, that he ever *entirely* fubdued the Decan. It is true, when he took the field, Conqueft attended him, and in his life-time his name was a terror to the Hindoo Chiefs of that country ; but we have feen that he was even under the neceffity of ftrengthening the power of the inferior leaders, in order to crufh the principal. The whole became his tributaries ; and all, I think, that can be further faid, with regard to his expeditions againft the Marattahs, is, that he weakened the ftate, by difmembering it, and making the intereft of individuals different from that of the whole collectively. Many of the prefent Jaghiredars are the defcendants of the chiefs by whole aid Aurungzebe got the better of Sewajie.

the

the year of the Hijera 1119 (A. D.
1707), when he died at Ahmudnegur, about fix years after he had reftored the Souraja to the territories of
his father.

On the death of Aurungzebe, the
army, that had for fome years kept
the Decan in order, fet out for Dhelli,
under the command of Affud Cawn,
to join the young prince and fucceffor
to the throne Bahadar Shaw, leaving
behind him the Mahrattah chiefs, and
ftrongly recommended it to Jaderow
and the others to be ready, on a fummons, to protect the diftricts of Ahmudnegur, Bejapoor, and Dowlatabad,
which lay contiguous to their different
Jaghires made over to them by Aurungzebe after the reduction of Sattarah.

The

The difputes betwixt the two fons of Aurungzebe Bahadar Shaw and Azim Shaw (relative to the fucceffion) threw the whole empire into confufion; for the governors of the different provinces were much divided in their opinion whom they fhould acknowledge as their fovereign, fome declaring for the elder, and fome for the younger brother. In the Decan, the governor of Bejapoor was one of the firft who revolted, and held out for Azim Shaw the younger.

Jaderow, with three other Mahrattah chiefs, were then lying near that capital; and on their remonftrating againft the governor's rebellion, he told them, that they were not acquainted with the Mogul conftitution, and perfifted in remaining in Azim

Shaw's

Shaw's intereft, on which they (the chiefs) refufed to pay any obedience to him, and immediately retired to their own Jaghires. The other chiefs of thefe people, who were ftationed near Ahmudnegur and Daulatabad, followed their example, all agreeing, that it was better to ftand aloof, till the diffentions betwixt the two brothers fhould ceafe, and one or the other be eftablifhed on the throne; for, by taking the part of either, they would likely incur the difpleafure, and feel the refentment of the conqueror, if unluckily they fhould have given af-fiftance to his opponent.

The contentions between the fons of Aurungzebe daily increafed the diftracted ftate of the Mogul empire; which furnifhed the family of the late

Se-

Sewajie with an excellent opportunity to revive that power and authority in the Decan, which they at one time poffeffed.

Azim Shaw, who on his father's death was in the government of Guzerat, being diffatisfied with fuch a patrimony, and thinking his right to the throne equal to his elder brother's, wrote to Bahadar Shaw on that fubject, and propofed to him an equal divifion of the empire, preparing, at the fame time, to enforce his pretenfions, fhould they not be admitted of. Bahadar Shaw refufing to comply with this demand, he fet out from Guzerat with an army of fifty thoufand men, and was met in the Malwar province by his brother, at the head of a large army, though

ftill

ftill inferior to that of Azim Shaw. Bahadar Shaw even then endeavoured, but in vain, to conciliate matters with his brother, whofe obftinacy at laft proved his ruin, as he was flain in the battle that enfued foon after the armies met.

The Rajah himfelf was only a young man at this period; but an uncle of his by the mother's fide, named Sumpatrow, an ambitious and artful man, determined not to lofe fo favourable a juncture of raifing the family to its former fplendor. For that purpofe he wrote to Jaderow, who has already been mentioned, defiring him to reflect with himfelf to whom it was he owed obedience, and the wealth he at prefent enjoyed; to forget what was paffed, and not

to

to hefitate to embrace fo favourable
an opening for reftoring and con-
firming the fon of his old mafter,
in the power from which the father
had fallen, and that the declining ftate
of the Mogul empire now favoured
every attempt which could be made
to effect fo defirable an end.

Jaderow, on receiving this folici-
tation, confulted with the other
chiefs what was to be done ; when
it was agreed, that they fhould go
to Sattarah, and liften to fuch terms
of accommodation as might be offered
to them by Sumpatrow, who, when
the interview took place, propofed
to them, that, if they would unite
their forces under the banner of the
Sourajah, acknowledging him as their
chief, in return for quitting their Jag-

F   hires,

hires, and following his fortune, they
fhould fhare amongft them two
thirds of the profits of their cam-
paigns, and from the other third
they fhould alfo have wherewith to
pay their troops.

Sumpatrow entered into this un-
profitable agreement from a view to
futurity, without weighing maturely
the confequences which might attend fo rafh a precedent, facrificing
every other confideration to that
one of reftoring and eftablifhing the
nominal authority of the Surajah;
and to this injudicious and fhort-fighted
policy is to be attributed, in a great
degree, that mode of government
which has fo long fubfifted with the
Mahrattahs, where the whole power
is lodged in the hands of the Pefhwa,

7   or

or firft minifter, with fome of the
principal Jaghire officers, as his council.

Matters being thus fettled, Jaderow, who as yet had declined openly
acknowledging the Sourajah, now
came to Sattarah, and joined his
ftandard. Bajerow, for his faithful
fervices to the Rajah's family, was promoted to the chief rank of this confederacy next to the Rajah himfelf; and
the firft incurfion of this junto was
into the Bejapoor country, which they
plundered and laid wafte, alledging
that they acted by the authority of
Bahadar Shaw, whom the governor
of that province would not acknowledge ; and finding there was no probability of an oppofition to their
inroads, they readily embraced fo

favourable

favourable an opportunity of ftrengthening their power, by getting poffeffion of many of the fmall forts near
Sattarah. They next fet out for
Hyderabad, and enriched themfelves
not a little by their depredations in
that quarter. Sumpatrow, who had
acted all along as guardian to his
nephew the young Rajah, judged it
political to entruft the whole manage-
ment of the fruits of their expeditions
to Jaderow, thinking, by this, the
more firmly to attach him, and the
other chiefs, to his intereft, in cafe
of a reverfe of fortune.

It was in thefe laft-mentioned excurfions, in which the Sourajah had
alfo accompanied them, that Badjerow
(father to Ragoubah) and his brother
Chimnajie firft began to be of any
confequence.

confequence. Thefe two were fons
of one Ballijeram, a Bramin and a
native of Sewurdun *, who had com-
manded a body of five hundred
horfe, in Sewajie's fervice : and was
remarkable for his fidelity to that
Rajah, when deferted by fo many of
his principal officers, as has already
been taken notice of.

Bahadar Shaw had not well got
rid of his turbulent brother Azim
Shaw (who, as has been mentioned,
was flain in battle) when he had complaints, from the Ameers, in the
Decan, of the diftreffed ftate of that
country, from the hoftile invafions of
the Mahrattahs, who had thus taken
advantage of the internal diffentions
in the Mogul empire, to raife the
low ftate of their own   Bahadar

Shaw was however guided intirely
(relative to the meafures he fhould
purfue with the Mahrattahs) by the
advice of his Vifier Affud Kawn, who
had good opportunities of knowing
thefe people, their manner of fighting, and what numbers they could
bring into the field, as he had accompanied Aurungzebe in his two expeditions
in thofe parts ; and the Vifier, who
was likewife thoroughly acquainted
with the Mogul government, and
knew well how thofe in power belonging to it were affected, wifely
judged it for his mafter's intereft,
which he had much at heart, not
to rifk (by a foreign and moft likely
fruitlefs expedition) what at any rate
muft be attended with a vaft expence,
the involving the empire in frefh
troubles

troubles before it had well recovered from thofe occafioned by the death of Aurungzebe. The king therefore made a merit of neceffity, and fet about accommodating matters with the Mahrattahs, in a manner, though in fome degree derogatory to his government, yet certainly at that time much more to its real advantage, fince he gained the friendfhip of a people who only could have been kept under fubjection by a ftanding force, much fuperior to any he could have afforded, at fo great a diftance from the heart of his dominions, with fafety to his government.

He ordered the Vifier to write to Jaderow, to defire his attendance at Dhelli, in order to fettle the difputes in an amicable way ; but that chief,

dread-

dreading the confequences of what had paffed, excufed himfelf, by pretending ficknefs : and the other officers, likewife, from the fame motives, declined undertaking the journey, which gave Bajerow the firft opportunity of raifing himfelf and family to that degree of fortune at which they afterwards arrived. This embaffy to Dhelli was no fooner propofed to him, than he chearfully undertook it, being naturally of an afpiring and ambitious genius : and, knowing life was all he could lofe ; whereas, fhould he fucceed, it would equally advance his reputation and fortune ; he accordingly fet out, about the year of the Hijera 1121, (A. D. 1709,) attended by his brother Chimnajie, and about 7000 men.

Jaderow,

Jaderow, in anfwer to the fummons he had received, excufed himfelf in the manner as already related ;
and at the fame time told the Vifier,
that the Mahrattahs had all agreed to
acknowledge and abide by the Rajah,
fon to their old and original chief Sewajie ; and, for his own part, he
had but little influence amongft them,
but thought it would be for the intereft of the Mogul government to
allow the Saw Rajah a chout from the
revenues of the Decan, which would
entirely put a ftop to their further ex-
ertions, urging alfo, in favour of this
demand, the grants they held before Aurungzebe's expeditions into
that country.

Bajerow, by his manner and addrefs, gained much the affection of
the

the King, which, amongst other caufes, had its weight in facilitating the bufinefs of his embaffy: the propofal was agreed to, after taking an obligation in the name of the Saw Rajah, that he fhould affift the King with what forces he could mufter, whenever his fervices might be demanded; the expences however of fuch expeditions to be defrayed by the King, exclufive of the chout.

Bajerow, after a fix months ftay at Dhelli, returned to Sattarah, where his reception was as favourable as he could wifh, and fuch as his fuccefs entitled him to. As a reward for the fervices had done the ftate, Sumpatrow and the Saw Rajah appointed him to the office of Purdawn, which is the fame as Pefhwa, or prime minifter. He

foon

foon after this fet out, with an army, to collect the firft fruits of his new grants, which he carried with him, to fhew to thofe on whofe diftricts they were given. The juftnefs of his claims being allowed, the Decan remained in peace and tranquillity the five or fix following years, which ter-minated the life of Bahadar Shaw, whofe death at laft occafioned frefh commotions in the empire, and once more gave an opportunity to the Mahrattahs to increafe their growing power.

Two fons of Bahadar Shaw, fol-lowing the example fet them at their grandfather's death, difputed the fucceffion, which had not been fet-tled by the late king. The eldeft, Jehandar Shaw, who was at Dhelli

at

at the time his father died, afcended the throne; the other fon, Azimoo Shaw, in Bahadar Shaw's time, had been appointed to the Subadaree of Bengal; but, alledging his pretenfions to the crown not to be inferior to his brother's, he fet out with a large army to enforce his claim.

Affud Cawn, on the death of the late king, retired from all public bufinefs, being now far advanced in years, and perceiving the difficulties he fhould have to encounter in managing the government, in oppofition to the parties formed contrary to its true intereft. Every thing therefore was carried on, in the name of the young king, by Seid Abdullah Cawn and Haffen Alli Cawn, two brothers, the one Vifier and

3

and the other Buckfhie. Thefe two, being informed of Azimoo Shaw's intention, prepared to oppofe it; and that they might the more eafily promote their own views, and pre-ferve the confequence they had ac-quired in the government, fent for Bajerow, who quickly arrived at Dhelli, with an army of about 12,000 men. His brother Chimnajie, kunta, and Peelajee (the laft grand-father to Fatty Sing) were three of his principal officers on this fervice,

The Mahrattahs were kept at Dhelli during Jehandar's expedition againft his brother, which foon ter-minated in his favour, by the en-tire defeat of Azimoo Shaw's army, that prince having with difficulty, faved himfelf by flight: nor did he

long

long furvive his difgrace, for he foon after died with grief.

This turn of fortune, however favourable it appeared at prefent to Jehander Shaw, was far, in its confequences; from having the defired effect ; for not long after this victory Furroockfeer, fon to Azimoo Shaw, a youth of about eighteen years of age, determined to revenge his father's death ; and, if poffible, to get himfelf fixed on the throne of Dhelli. Though he met with oppofition at firft, yet fuccefs foon attended him : for, having defeated his uncle, who fled from the field of battle, he was thereon immediately feated on the mufnud, and all the honours of Majefty paid him, but the whole power of government remained in the

the hands of the two minifters, Ab-
doollah Kawn and Haffen Alli Kawn,
who were ftrongly fufpected of fa-
vouring his promotion *, and their
continued authority was deemed the
ftipulated reward for their fervice; fo
that Furroockfeer was then, and for
feveral years after, nothing more
than an inftrument in their hands to
promote their own ambition ; for as
foon as he arrived at the years of ma-
turity, and became fenfible of his
fituation, they did not long hefitate
what ftep fhould be taken, in order
to fecure their own power, which

---

* I believe it is in Dow's Hiftory of Hindof
tan that this revolution is pofitively faid to have
been originally fchemed, and finally accomplifhed, by thefe two artful and ambitious minifters. The general view which is here given
of their government ferves to confirm the
affertion.

they

they faw would decline as the young king advanced in life. They therefore depofed and imprifoned him; and taking Mahomed Shaw, fon to Jehawn Shaw, from his confinement, raifed him to the regal dignity. It was immediately after the Revolution in favour of Furroockfeer, that Bajerow rendered the moft effential fervice to the Mahrattah ftate; which he effected in the following manner.

As all places of truft and employment in the Mogul government were at that time beftowed on the favourites of the two minifters, who had placed the king himfelf upon the throne; the Subadaree of the Decan was given to Allum Allie Kawn, one of their nephews; and there being no further occafion for the fervice of

the

the Mahrattahs near Dhelli, the young Subadar was fent to his go-vernment, under the protection of Bajerow, who was particularly de-fired to fupport and affift him in his new authority. Bajerow, whom thefe two minifters wifhed to keep in their intereft, was at this time offered a Jaghire in the Decan; but though it cannot be fuppofed his refufal pro-ceeded from difintereftednefs, yet it is faid he then declined accepting the offer; giving them to underftand, he had a petition to make in behalf of the Saw Rajah.

This petition imported nothing lefs than a grant of a chout from the province of Bengal, Poorub, Malva, and Guzerat; and the two minifters, knowing the inftability of their own

G   upftart

upftart and ill-acquired power, and
dreading the influence and envy of
thofe who were debarred from fhar-
ing it with them, were determined
to omit nothing, however deftruc-
tive to the intereft, and derogatory
to the honour of the empire, to fecure the ruling of it intirely to themfelves ; they therefore, in complying
with this exorbitant demand, may
be faid to have given the finifhing
ftroke to the power of the Mogul
empire in Hindoftan, which began
to decline on the death of Aurungzebe. To this alfo is to be attributed the ftrength and flourifhing
condition to which the Mahrattah
ftate foon after arrived. Another
reafon affigned for the ruin of the
Mogul empire, and the quick rife of
the

the Mahrattah, is likewife imputed to the maladminiftration of this reign.

It had been a cuftom eftablifhed by one of the Mogul emperors in Hindoftan, before Aurungzebe, to receive an annual tribute, or tax, from the Hindoos in every part of Hindoftan where the Mogul government exifted ; every houfe paid fo much, according to the reputed wealth of the owner; and as very few of the cafts, or tribes, were exempted from this impofition, it was the fource of immenfe riches to the treafury.

The Rajah of Oodapoor, Jaifing Sewajie, had a daughter famed for her beauty all over India. Furrock-feer, hearing fo much of her charms, determined to procure, if poffible, fo

amiable

amiable an acquifition to his Seraglio. He difclofed his intention to his two favourites, who, always glad of any thing to withdraw his attention from affairs of government, moft readily acquiefced; and overtures were accordingly made to the father of the young lady, who, after fome fcruples, confented to give her in marriage to the king, on thefe three conditions being fulfilled, viz. That the tax fo long impofed on the Hindoos fhould from henceforth be relinquifhed; that the country of Oodapoor fhould be no longer tributary to the Mogul; and that none but his defcendents fhould be fupported in their pretenfions to the Rajahfhip of Oodapoor. Thefe ftipulations being agreed to, and figned

by

by the king, the marriage foon after took place.

Bajerow, after he had arrived in the Decan, and fettled Allum Allie Kawn at Aurungabad, returned to Sattarah, with ftill greater eclat than from his former expedition; nor, in managing his mafter's intereft, had he been neglectful of his own; for, notwithftanding his feeming patriotic fpirit, when a Jaghire was offered to him, it is certain, that at the fame time he received the grants for the chouts in the four provinces already mentioned in the name of his mafter, he was likewife in his own name furnifhed by the fame authority with the proper papers for his taking poffeffion of Bhimrie, Culliany, and Sewardun, which yielded

G 3   upwards

upwards of three lacks of Rupees
annually. Bajerow's return to the
Decan with Allum Allie Kawn was
about the year of the Hijera 1122
(A. D. 1710). Having paid a vifit to
his new Jaghires, and finifhed what
bufinefs he had to do there, he returned to Aurungabad, to wait the
orders of the new Subadar.

Every thing remained without
any material change with regard to
the Mogul government for about fix
or feven years after Bajerow's return
to the Decan, when Furrockfeer
(who has been already alluded to)
was confined*, and Mahomed Shaw
placed

* Confining the Emperor did not fatisfy thefe
more than ambitious ufurpers; fear and refentment operated fo ftrongly as actuated them
to aggravate their former crimes by the com-
miffion of others of an infinitely more heinous
nature.

placed on the Muffmud: two years
had fcarce elapfed of this new reign,
when a change of miniftry at Dhelli
threw the whole empire once more

nature. Shocking to relate, this unhappy fovereign had fcarcely loft his crown, when he
was likewife deprived of his fight in the moft
cruel manner by red hot wire being drawn
acrofs his eyes. Even this deplorable fituation
did not foften the unfeeling hearts of his im-
placable enemies; but his murder, by their
commands, foon terminated his fufferings. There
were two emperors on the Mogul throne betwixt Furroockfeer and Mahomed Shaw; but
their reigns were fo fhort, and fo little interest-
ing, that hiftory makes hardly more mention of
them than juft their acceffion and death. Raf-
fee-ul-denjah and Raffee-ul dowlat, two brothers, coufins to the laft emperor, on whofe
death the firft of thefe was taken from his confinement, and placed on the Muffnud; but his
exalted fituation only haftened his end; for
thofe who had raifed him permitted him to live
but a few months. His brother was proclaimed
his fucceffor; but a natural death, within a
week or little more of his promotion, in all
probability faved him from the miferable fate
of his two predeceffors, and made way for
Mahomed Shaw.

G 4   into

into confufion, which, as ufual, proved in the end of great advantage
to the Mahrattahs, who were never
fcrupulous in efpoufing the caufe that
was moft likely to promote the wel-
fare of their own ftate ; nor were
they long in difcovering what fide
would be moft conducive to its intereft, at leaft to its temporary aggran-
dizement.

The adminiftration of the Mogul
government was now lodged in the
hands of a number of the nobility
who had formed themfelves into a
confederacy againft the two brothers
Haffen Allie Kawn and Abdullah
Kawn, long fince rendered obnoxious
to them, by monopolizing the fole
authority to themfelves, and accumulating wealth, which others thought

3   them-

themselves, and in fact were, much better entitled to. These two brothers fell victims to their own ambition.

Nizamal Muluck, who had been the principal in bringing about this Revolution, was, immediately after it, with the entire consent of the other grandees, appointed first minister of the empire; but the volatile disposition of the young king (who was much addicted to pleasures of every sort), being so very unconsonant to his serious turn of mind *,

which

* However trifling the following anecdote appears, yet it may not be improper to insert it, since it seems a corroborating circumstance to this part of the narrative.

It is said, that at an exhibition of some monkeys of a remarkable size, who had been taught to dance and play a number of odd tricks; the king, who delighted in even the lowest amusements, was highly pleased with the agility and readiness of these animals; one

of

which was ever intent on bufinefs,
and forefeeing the troubles which
oppofition to the prince's inclination,
encouraged by fo many of the young
courtiers, would probably involve him
in, he judged it beft policy for himfelf to make ufe of the influence he
then held at court, to fecure fome-
thing at a diftance from it, which
would more likely contribute to his

of them in particular (an old one) attracted his
notice; and addreffing Nizamal Muluck, with
a fignificant fneer on his countenance, defired
him to obferve how the *old monkey* jumped
about : this vulgar witticifm (from the manner
it was fpoke) occafioned a laugh, and was matter of merriment to the other courtiers who were
ftanding by; but it had a very different effect
on the Vifier, who, imagining the king alluded
to him (being at this time advanced in life),
received it as the higheft infult, and (as the
ftory goes) determined, from that moment, to
leave the court, where he had for fome time
obferved diffipation and depravity of manners
fo much to prevail.

inde-

independence than the high office he
held : for the diffolute manners of
the court, which made his prefent
fituation fo irkfome to him, likewife
gave him reafon to believe, that, if
he was once fixed in a diftant province
of the empire, he might purfue with
impunity fuch meafures as he might
conceive moft conducive to promote
his own ambition ; he therefore, in
a little time after he had come to the
head of affairs, on pretence of Allum
Allie Kawn's youth and inexperience,
which he faid would be taken advantage of by the Mahrattahs, to the great
difgrace and detriment of the empire, procured from the king the Sunnuds of the government of the Decan
to himfelf, and fet out with an army
of only 12,000 men for that province ;

vince; delivering over his charge as
Viſier to Camer Oodeen Kawn, a relation of his own, who, he was ſure,
would, on all occaſions, aſſiſt him in
his views.

Allum Allie Kawn, being adviſed
of what was going on at the Mogul
court, and knowing how ſoon it was
likely to affect him in his government, made every preparation for the
reception of Nizamal Muluck, on
whoſe approach he ſent his Buckſhie,
Delawar Kawn, and Bajerow, who
ſtill adhered to his intereſt, to attack
him on his march. An engagement
was brought on near Barampoor, in
which Allum Alli Kawn's Buckſhie
was killed, and his army, in conſequence, although ſuperior in numbers

bers to his opponents, entirely defeated.

Bajerow, after this, inftead of returning to Allum Allie Kawn, to affift him in his future operations,
went to Sattarah, where letters from
Nizamal Mulick to the Saw Rajah
foon arrived; fetting forth the folly
of oppofing him in the execution of
his orders from the court of Dhelli;
that he came with no hoftile inten-
tions; nor would the peace of the
Decan have been interrupted, had Allum Allie Kawn quietly refigned his
government. But the fureft and moft
effectual means he knew to fecure the
Mahrattahs to his intereft were the
promifes of a confirmation of the
chout which had been granted to
them in the former reign, together
with

with an addition to Bajerow's Jaghire from his own province, befides paying the expences of their army when employed by him.

Bheer, a fmall Purgunnah in the Decan, yielding about three lack of rupees annually, was the place now ceded to Bajerow. Thefe terms were too flattering to both the Rajah and his Premier to be rejected.

Bajerow accordingly joined Nizamal Muluck with all poffible fpeed at Barampoor, where he ftill waited, in hopes that Allum Allie Kawn would, without further refiftance, fubmit himfelf to his fortune : but in this he was much difappointed, fince Ameer, knowing he had nothing to expect from the prefent Mogul adminiftration, was determined to follow the

5   ex-

example of his friends at Dhelli, who had fallen in oppofing it*, and refign his government only with his life. He therefore, in lefs than a fortnight after the defeat of his Buckfhie, advanced himfelf from Aurungabad, at the head of 30,000 men, towards Barampoor, where, notwithftanding the remonftrances of Nizamal Mulick and his adherents, he perfifted in refifting that Vifier to the laft; but in

---

* The two brothers, Haffen Allie Cawn and Abdullah Cawn, are here particularly alluded to. We have feen a fhort fketch of their hiftory, and it is here only requifite to notice their exit. The firft met his death by a confpiracy formed againft him; the latter foon after was taken prifoner, and died of the wounds he received in oppofing the confederacy of the other nobles: he had a confiderable party in his favour, and had ftrengthened it by a number of mercenaries; but was ftill inferior to the force of his opponents, who were headed by the emperor himfelf; at leaft his prefence with them gave an appearance of the royal fanction to all their proceedings.

every

every fkirmifh, which hapened almoft
daily for near a month, he was defeated ; and in the end his own death,
which he met on the field of battle,
terminated the difpute, and eftablifhed tranquillity in the Decan. This
was the firft time that Nizamal Muluck experienced the fervice of Baja-
row, whom, with his troops, he employed in preventing provifions coming to Allum Allie Kawn's camp; a
fervice particularly fuited to a body of
Mahrattahs.   Thefe circumftances
happened in the Decan about the
year of the Hijera 1132, (A. D.
1719.)

Soon after Nizamal Muluck was fettled at Aurungabad the Sawrajah
himfelf, with a number of a Mahrattah chiefs, came to pay their obei-
fance

fance to him. He was received by
that Subah with many marks of dif-
tinction, according to the cuftoms of
the country.

For near eighteen years after this
change of government in the Decan
the Mahrattahs made no attempt
to difturb its peace; but there, as
well as in the other provinces of the
Mogul empire from whofe revenues
they were intitled to a chout, they
received it regularly by the officers
appointed for that purpofe, till the
invafion of Nadir Shaw *, which threw
the

* After the feveral hiftories which have appeared of this extraordinary man, and his invafion of Hindoftan in the year 1738, it would
be prefumptuous, as it is needlefs, to attempt
accounting for, or elucidating that matter here.
The readers who wifh to perufe the hiftory of
the event alluded to, will have their curiofity
moft

the empire again into the moſt diftracted condition, and afforded thoſe
people freſh opportunities of exten-
ding and ſtrengthening the power
which had, by this time, become ſo

moſt fully ſatisfied by reading " The Life of
" Nadir Shaw," publiſhed in 1773, by Mr.
Jones. Though that Gentleman's fame as a
ſcholar and man of genius can receive no addi-
tional luſtre from any encomium of mine, and
therefore I attempt none; yet I cannot content
myſelf by thus ſimply mentioning his name,
without at the ſame time acknowledging, that
it is to a very beneficial part of his literary la-
bours (his Perſian Grammar) I am much in-
debted for what ſmall knowledge of the Perſian
language I have acquired. Nor are thoſe who
are deſirous of making any proficiency in the
Perſian and Arabic tongues leſs obliged to Mr.
Richardſon, for his Dictionary and Arabic Grammar. Such aids to ſo uſeful a branch of learn-
ing have been long wanting. The Eaſt India
Company at large, and individuals in their ſer-
vice in particular, have the greateſt obligations
to theſe two gentlemen, who have ſo well ſucceeded in removing the obſtacles to the application for this attainment.

for-

formidable as to be feared and courted all over India.

Nizamal Muluck, who, it is faid, contributed fo much to facilitate Nadir Shaw's conqueft of Hindoftan, fet out for Dhelli, in order to be prefent at an event of fuch confequence as that prince's approach was likely to produce. On his departure from the Decan he left his fon Nazir Jung in charge of that government, with but a fmall body of troops; as he fuppofed, from the ftate of tranquillity to which he had brought it, partly by force, and partly by treaties with, and grants to, its former difturbers, that there was little to be apprehended from them. But in the courfe of a few months Nazir Jung (though victorious) had convincing proofs of the error of

H 2   this

this conjecture; for no fooner had
the Mahrattahs certain intelligence
of Nadir Shaw's fuccefs, than they
began to form their fchemes of profiting by the general confufion; and the
report that prevailed of Nadir Shaw's
difpofition towards Nizamal Muluck,
for his treachery to his old mafter,
was alfo favourable to their views.

Bajerow accordingly marched towards Aurungabad, at the head of
an army of 15,000 horfe, and encamped near the capital; he fent
an infolent letter to Nazir Jung,
importing, that fince Nadir Shaw was
now on their throne of the Mogul
empire, the Mahrattahs (the ancient
Zemindars) of this country owed
no longer obedience to the Subah of
the Decan, at leaft till he fhould be
provided

provided with frefh Sunnuds from
the new emperor; and that he therefore muft abandon Aurungabad,
and repair to Dhelli, for that purpofe. A demand likewife was made
for the fum of eight Lacks of Rupees,
to be paid immediately, as a Nal-
bundie * to the Saw Rajah ; and a

* The name of a tax impofed on pretence of
keeping the horfes in fhoes, as the word itfelf
denotes—*Nalbund,* in the country language,
fignifying a black-fmith ; and *Nalbundna* to
fhoe a horfe. This impofition is often a very
heavy one, as it rather depends on the difcre-
tion and humanity of thofe who collect it, than
forming part of the revenues of the ftate ; for it
is to be obferved, that this and fimilar extor-
tions are not confined to the enemy's country
alone, but friends and foes equally feel the hand
of oppreffion from the rapacious foldiery of an
Indian army, when headed by their own officers,
whofe conduct in general, as it ferves more to
increafe than alleviate the unavoidable horrors
of war, is feldom fuch, to the fubjects of thofe
who employ them, as to render lefs grievous
the burthens of an arbitrary government.

H 3   chal-

challenge to the field of battle, in cafe of non-compliance, accompanied this letter. Nazir Jung, on this occafion, called a council of war, confifting of eight of his principal officers, by whofe fidelity and intrepidity he could only expect fuccefs in oppofing the enemy. They affured him, that while they had life they would zealoufly contribute all in their power to preferve the dignity of the Mogul government, and punifh thofe who were now infulting it.

Nazir Jung, with an army of near 20,000 men, in a fhort time accordingly left the city, to face Bajerow. Both parties met ; and, after obftinate fkirmifhes for feveral days together, the Mahrattahs were obliged

to

to retreat to a confiderable diftance. They were followed however by Nazir Jung and his conquering army, and had fcarce time to reft themfelves till they reached the plains of Poonah, where Bajerow, notwith-ftanding the ftrongeft remonftrances of his officers, was determined to rifk a battle. Nazir Jung's army, from their former fuccefs, and the enco-miums of their leader, accompanied with liberal donations as an encourage-ment to their valour, continued the purfuit with the greateft fpirits; and every appearance gave Nazir Jung room to expect the fuccefs which foon attended him. When he was advanced to the plains of Poonah, he found Bajerow's army drawn out, ready to receive him; an engagement

foon

foon began, and was fupported on each fide with equal vigour for fome length of time, till the lofs of four of Bajerow's principal officers, who fell in the action, too evidently promifed the victory to his enemies. Bajerow, irritated at his fate, and borne away with grief and defpair at the confequences which fo foon attended the death of thefe leaders, at firft feemed carelefs of life; and perfonal courage was the only quality of a general which he difcovered, in order to repair the misfortune; for he rufhed with fury into the thickeft of the battle, where he encountered Timur Cawn, an officer of deftinction with Nazir Jung, who, evading the ftroke of a fabre

which

which Bajerow made at him, ſtun-
ned his antagoniſt to the ground
with the blow of a battle-axe. Bajerow, recovering from this, made
little more reſiſtance to his deſtiny, but
fled from the field of battle, which
was yet bravely diſputed by his brother, Chimnajie; who, at laſt, finding his troops thrown into confuſion
and overpowered on every quarter,
was obliged to follow his brother's
example, and thereby compleat the
victory of Nazir Jung. It was reported that Bajerow propoſed to collect what he could of his broken army, and make another ſtand at Tilli-
gaum. Nazir Jung ſoon made his
appearance at that place; but, being
informed that the enemy had taken
the

the road to Bhoorgaut*, he continued
his purfuit to this pafs; but here he
received intelligence, that Bajerow
and Chimnajie had defcended by the
Paigaut † to Cullianie and Bhimrie ‡.

As Bajerow had always been highly
refpected for a warrior, and juftly
confidered to have rendered, on former occafions, the moft effential fervices to the Mahrattah State ; which,
for near twenty-two years, he managed with fame to himfelf, and to
the fatisfaction of his countrymen; fo

* The name of a pafs (large enough for
cattle, artillery, &c.) in thofe mountains, which
divides the Decan from the low country towards
the fea coaft on the Malabar fide of India, com-
monly called the Cockun.

† Another pafs, but only a foot-path, as
the word in the language of the country im-
plies.

‡ Bajerow's Jaghires, two places of importance in the Cockun.

5   this

this difgrace made the deeper impref-
fion on his mind ; he furvived it but
fix or feven months, and during that
time could never be prevailed on to
vifit his mafter the Saw Rajah, who
invited him to Sattarah by a letter
written in the moft delicate terms, im-
puting his defeat entirely to bad fortune, which often attends the wifeft
meafures.

Nazir Jung, having pillaged and
burnt Poonah, and the town of Sattarah, returned to Aurungabad, famed for his victory, and loaded with
the fpoils of the enemy. He rewarded handfomely the troops who
contributed fo much to his fuccefs,
and iffued his orders throughout the
Decan for a ftop to be put to the

pay-

payment of the chout to the Mahrattahs.

Bajerow left three fons. Ballajierow, the eldeft, fucceeded his father,
as Pefhwa to the Saw Rajah; and
under him, as will appear in the
fequel, the Mahrattah ftate recovered
the fhock it had fo lately received by
his father's overthrow, and arrived at
the higheft pitch of power we have
yet feen it.

The imbecillity of the Mogul
government, which had been fo favourable to his anceftors, likewife
continued to facilitate the fchemes
of Ballajerow; for the extention of
the Mahrattah influence in India,
till the fatal expedition to Dhelli,
and the lofs of the battle of Pannyput, about twenty years ago, en-

7   tirely

tirely changed the face of affairs,
and may be noted as the æra of
the commencement of its decline,
notwithstanding the formidable appearance some recent transactions
denote; for, as a state, we find, in
a few years after this event, those
in whom the government was vest-
ed, divided amongst themselves, and
resembling too much, by their internal diffentions, that unwieldy empire
on whose ruin they had raised their
own.

But to return to the narrative.
When Nizamal Muluck was informed of his son's success in fruftrating
the hostile attempts of the Saw Rajah and Bajerow, he was highly
pleafed with the whole of his conduct; and, on his return to the

Decan

Decan (after Nadir Shaw had re-efta-
blifhed the Mogul), amply rewarded
the chiefs of his army for their
adherence and affiftance to Nazir Jung.
Nizamal Muluck, though exafperat-
ed at the bafenefs of the Mahrattahs,
yet he was fenfible of the neceffity
of retaining in his fervice fome of
their principal leaders, with their
adherents ; and thereby dividing a
force, which, if united, would ever
be dangerous to his dominions. But
inftead of Ballajierow, he fent for
and appointed Ragoojie Bhoonfla, Rajah of Nagpoor, for what fervices he
might in future have occafion to
employ the Mahrattahs upon. Though
this chief was related to the Saw
Rajah, yet the preference Nizamal
Muluck naturally gave him was by
no

no means pleafing to the latter, who, befides his juft partiality to Bajerow's family, probably dreaded the increafing power of fo diftant a branch of his own. This preference feems to have been the caufe of the enmity that is ftill faid to fubfift betwixt that family and Ragounathrow *. Piqued, however, as both the Saw Rajah and Ballajie were, they were not now in a condition to oppofe the will of the Subah of the Decan.

Ballajie remained quiet about Sattarah and Poonah for fome years, repairing, as much as poffible, the devaftations which followed his father's

* Ragounathrow, or Ragoubah, the Chief whofe pretenfions to the Mahrattah Government involved the Englifh in the war they now maintain with that State.

dif-

difafters; determined however to ufe his utmoft efforts to retrieve them the firft favourable opportunity that might offer. Nor was it long ere the death of Nizamal Mulick gave him encouragement to hope for fuccefs. That Subah died, when about one hundred years of age, at Barrampoor, in 1748. He was fucceeded in the government of the Decan by the abovenamed Nazir Jung (Gazoodie Cawn, his eldeft fon being at Dhelli), who, as well as his father, faw that the Mahrattahs would be a dangerous rival in power to him, if care were not taken to prevent their uniting and recovering the blow they had received, therefore would never either take the Saw Rajah, or his minifter Ballajie Row, into favour again.

It

It was foon after Nazir Jung's acceffion to the Mufnud of the Decan
that the Saw Rajah died. But, before
his death, in prefence of Ballajie Row,
and a numerous Mujlifs, or affembly
of other Mahrattah chiefs and officers,
he appointed the fon of a Bramin
(whom he had adopted as his own)
to be his fucceffor, by the title of
Ram Rajah, who was however at this
time but a boy, and confequently all
matters of government, as well as the
executive power, became more than
ever vefted in the Pefhwa or Prime
Minifter.

Ballajie Row's abilities being allowed by all concerned in the manage-
ment of affairs, and the attachment
likewife which was well known to
have fubfifted betwixt his family and

I   the

the old Rajah's ftill remaining, every one was ready to promote what political principles he judged proper to adopt for the good of the ftate, and affift him in the execution thereof.

Nazir Jung, fhortly after his father's death, fet out on an expedition to fettle the Carnatic; yet during that Subah's life his power was too formidable for the Mahrattahs to rifk the incurring his difpleafure by any further hoftile incurfions. Secret preparations for taking the advantage of fuch favourable events as might occur were all that could be done at this time; but foon the unhappy cataftrophe* which befell Nazir Jung at

* The reader will find a particular and diftinct account of this horrid tranfaction in Mr. Orme's juftly admired Hiftory of the war in India.

Gingee,

Gingee, where he was treacherouf-
ly murdered by thofe whom he
deemed the moft faithful in his
caufe, afforded the long-wifhed-for
opportunity.

Ballajie Row, to repair the misfortune of the ftate, and indulge
likewife his own ambitious views, as
foon as he heard of Nazir Jung's death,
determined to take the field with what
troops he could mufter, and levy
contributions throughout the Decan,
which was now in no condition to
refift him. Accompanied with Suddabah Toollajie Holcur, and feveral
other chiefs, he accordingly fet out
at the head of 15,000 men, and
went directly to Aurungabad, where
he obliged the wife of Nazir Jung to
give him fifteen Lack of Rupees;

which,

which, however, was only part of
a greater demand; for the hopes of
benefiting effentially, either by ap-
pearing to have fupported the family of the Subah, fhould it reco-
ver its confequence, or, at any rate,
to avail himfelf of its fall, induced
him not only to forbear urging a
further demand at prefent, but likewife led him to be the more eafily
prevailed on to repair to the affiftance
of Nizam Ally and Sallabat Jung, for
whofe fafety, after Nazir Jung's death,
much was to be feared.

Whenever the critical fituation of
a neighbouring power affords a probability of gaining an advantage, the
Mahrattahs feldom overlook the opportunity; though in this inftance
they were rather premature: and
we

we fee them here, as in other periods of their hiftory, fall into that
error fo common in ftates where war
is the chief profeffion, and commer-
cial views form no part of their
political pinciples, more ready to
fnatch with eagernefs at whatever
bids fair for immediate aggrandize-
ment and accumulating wealth, than
planning and purfuing fuch meafures as are adapted for procuring
and maintaining more folid advantages.

Ballajie Row accordingly left Aurungabad ; but, intent on profiting
at all events by the expedition, he
began by levying fupplies through
the country as he went; and about
Hyderabad, and the adjacent diftricts,
it is faid, he collected near twenty

Lacks

Lacks of Rupees, for the Zemindars and Pattels, finding he had forcibly received a confiderable amount from that city, knew that nothing remained for them but implicit obedience to what impofitions he chofe to exact.

His hopes, however, as we fhall hereafter fee, were foon fruftrated by a more favourable turn to Nizam Ally's affairs than he had expected, for, while he was thus employed, advices were received of the two brothers having defeated the Afghans *.

Fei-

---

* Or Pitans, a race of Mahometans inhabiting the Northern provinces of India on the borders of Perfia, and faid to be originally converts from the Hindoo religion. They are a bold and warlike people; but fincerity is not a virtue often afcribed to them. Thofe of them here alluded to were the Nabobs, or feudatory Chiefs (by birth of that tribe) in Nazir Jung's army, who

Feizoolla Cawn, then governor of Hyderabad, wrote a congratulatory epiftle to his mafter on this victory, and did not forget to give him an account of Ballajie's conduct, and the confequences of it, in thefe parts.

Nizam Ally, as may well be fup-pofed, did not mean to pafs over with impunity the advantage taken of his abfence to diftrefs his defence-lefs fubjects; nor were his threats long unknown to Ballajie Row, whofe Vakeel, in Nizam Ally's army, fent him the earlieft notice of fuch occur-rences as might particularly affect him. The Mahrattahs were now near Ado-nilachore; but Ballajie Row, not thinking himfelf ftrong enough to

who confpired againft his life. The reader has been told, in a previous note, where informa-tion on this fubject is fully to be found.

wait

wait the enemy's approach, returned to Sattarah, where he lodged the fruits of his depredations.

Nizam Ally and Sallabat Jung returned, by the way of Barrampoor, towards Poonah, which they plundered and laid waſte ; and, after having the fifteen Lack of Rupees, which Ballajie Row had exacted from Aurungabad, refunded to them, they purſued their route to that capital. The renown of theſe two brothers was now become ſo great, that for three or four years after this ſucceſs the Decan was permitted to enjoy the bleſſings of peace. But this interval of repoſe ſeems to have been dedicated only by the reſtleſs Mahrattahs to preparations to enforce future demands ; for, as ſoon as the late

I   de··

devaſtation in and about Poonah was in a tolerable degree repaired, Balla-jie Row, as alſo the other Mahrattah chiefs, piqued with reſentment at the humiliating condition to which they had been driven, ſet ſeriouſly about providing for a retaliation. The treaſury was at this time low; but the inconveniencies ariſing there-from were removed by the help of a very rich Bramin of NaſſickTrimmuck, who, at the repeated ſollicitations of the principal conductors of the propo-ſed enterprize (which they urged was in the cauſe of religion), was perſua-ded to riſk almoſt his whole fortune (near half a Crore of Rupees); and Bal-lajie Row himſelf, with the other leaders, made up what further ſup-plies were requiſite before they could

venture

venture to engage openly in the premeditated ſcheme. A Crore of Rupees being collected, Ballajie Row began augmenting his forces; and in eight months the Mahrattah army was 50,000 ſtrong in cavalry only, with which he loſt no time to invade Nizam Ally's territories, demanding an immediate reſtitution of the fifteen Lack of Rupees which he had been obliged to return.

Nizam Ally and his brother Sallabat Jung had taken the field on the firſt intimation of the Mahrattahs approach; and now both armies being encamped near Ahmudnagur, Nizam Ally, perceiving that he would not be able to cope with the force he had to oppoſe, ſent overtures of accommodation to the Mahrattah.

rattah chief. But Ballajie Row, finding his ftrength fuperior to that of his
enemy, his anfwers only befpoke a de-
termination to enforce his demands,
fhould they not be otherwife complied
with. This brought on fome very
warm and frequent fkirmifhes. Still
nothing decifive was the confequence,
till a manoeuvre propofed by a Suddabah *, and agreed to by Ballajie Row
and the other chiefs, produced the
defired effect. It was this: About
a third of their army was detached
to plunder and lay wafte feveral
Purgunnahs of the Decan, which
they knew had no troops left for
their defence, and which moftly
belonged to Nizam Ally's officers,

* A nephew of Ballajie Row's. See the more
particular account of this family at the end of
the narrative.

who

who confequently were particularly
affected by the depredations the
Mahrattahs were making in their
Jagheers; they therefore remonftrat-
ed with their leader on the neceffity
of concluding a peace.

Nizam Ally had no other re-
fource but compliance. And one
great objection which ftood in the
way, namely, the payment of the
fifteen Lack of Rupees, was removed by the Jagheerdars, to whom
collectively it was · but of little importance, in comparifon to the lof-
fes they would otherwife fuftain,
befides the danger of the Mahrattahs
getting poffeffion of their different
forts.

Shawnawaz Cawn was accordingly
fent from Nizam Ally with frefh pro-
pofals,

pofals, and at all events to accommodate matters with Ballajie Row. The Chout being granted, and other demands likewife complied with, the two armies quitted the field, the Mahrattah for Poonah, and the Mogul for Aurungabad.

On Ballajie Row's return to Poonah he wifhed to difband a great part of his troops which had been retained for this laft fervice, on account of the vaft expence incurred by fo large an army. This impolitic meafure, however, was wifely oppofed by the other chiefs, as it would have rifked the lofs of every advantage the ftate had fo recently acquired, by inducing Nizam Ally to attempt retrieving what he had loft. And in order to raife frefh

fup-

fupplies, an expedition was fet on foot againft Hyder Naig's * dominions, which again involved the Mahrattahs, and the Subdah of the Decan, in frefh troubles ; for Hyder complained to Nizam Ally, as chief Lord of that whole country, but he had foon reafon to repent efpoufing Hyder's caufe ; for difgrace, and the moft

---

* Better known by the name of Hyder Allie, the famous ufurper of the fovereignty of the Maiffore country, and may be confidered in that principality as the Pefhwa has fo long been in the Mahrattah State, who, though he acknowledges a fuperior, takes care to preferve every power and authority in his own hands ; for, if my information is right, there is ftill a nominal Rajah of that kingdom. Hyder Allie is a perfonage pretty well known in the hiftory of Englifh politicks in India ; and it would much exceed the limits of an elucidating note to a work of this nature (which in itfelf is only meant to convey a general kind of knowledge) to give a particular account of a man who has made, and ftill continues to make, fo confpicuous a figure in Eaftern hiftory.

3

mor-

mortifying conceffions, were the confequence. When he found his inferiority in ftrength to the Mahrattahs,
and that his army was fuffering every
diftrefs, being pent up in a fituation
from which it could neither extricate
itfelf, nor receive fupplies of any
kind, he would gladly have compro-
mifed matters, by an offer of forty
Lack of Rupees; which not being
accepted of, upwards of double that
fum was promifed. But an extent
of territory was now become the
object of the Mahrattahs; and at laft
the Fort of Ahmudnagur, together
with Naffick Trimmuck, diftricts
which brought an annual revenue of
thirty Lack of Rupees, were put into
Ballajie Row's poffeffion.

What-

Whatever claims of tribute the Mahrattahs had from time to time acquired by force of arms, this feems to be the firft inftance where we find them obliging the Subahs of the Decan to yield them in form the abfolute right of any part of the Mogul Dominions. Thefe conceffions were made near Bedur. Nizam Ally returned to Aurungabad, mortified with his fate, and meditating revenge.

Ballajie Row, on the other hand, exulting in his fuccefs, only thought of embracing every opportunity that might give him a frefh opening to extend his conquefts. Scarce a twelvemonth had elapfed, when a circumftance fell out which afforded fubject of contention for that turbulent and impatient fpirit with which both were

ani-

animated. Nizam Ally had 150 horfes of a high value coming from Surat to Aurungabad. Ballajie Row, hearing of this, gave directions for their being intercepted, and brought to Poonah, which was accordingly done. They were demanded, but in vain; and this infult occafioned the renewal of war. Nizam Ally took the field, and haftened to Barrampoor, where Ballajie Row and his army then were. Ballajie Row, by the help of his fpies, foon had information at what part of the enemy's camp the tumbrels of powder were placed, and found means to fet fire to them in the night; when befides the prodigious havock which the explofion occafioned, the flames communicaing to the tents, fpread a con-

K   fternation

fternation through the whole encampment but too favourable to the general attack which Ballajie Row had planned, for at this time his horfe charged with fury. The fire fo frightened the elephants in the camp of Nizam Ally that they broke loofe and crufhed under foot wher-ever they went, adding not a little to the terror that prevailed. There was no oppofing the enemy, the attack was fo fudden, and the difmay fo univerfal. The affault began about midnight; and when day appeared, Ballajie drew off his forces, who by this time were glutted with flaughter, and left a fcene of mifery and devaftation not to be defcribed.

From the advantages now gained, others of a more permanent and

im-

important nature were foon effected.

Nizam Ally's troops had fuffered
too much to attempt any thing of-
fenfive ; the lofs of ammunition and
ftores likewife gave them every thing
to dread ; the enemy were numerous,
and had the command of the whole
country, which rendered abortive
every effort to repair the damage fuf-
tained by fire and fword.

Before the expiration of a month,
terms of accommodation were finally fettled. It was ftipulated, that
Barrampoor, and the whole province
of Kandefs, fhould be yielded up
to the conqueror, who took care to
have the treaty put in execution before the two armies feparated. All
the governors on the part of Nizam

Ally

Ally were therefore removed, and thofe of Ballajie Row took poffeffion.

By this Narrative it appears, that the peace which this laft mentioned treaty had produced was likewife but of a very fhort duration.

The perfidy of Shanawaz Cawn*, Dewan to Nizam Ally, laid the

* When in India I had in my poffeffion a poem in the Moorifh language, on the fubject of Nazir Jung's affaffination at Gingee, and which is faid to have been written by a perfon well acquainted with the different actors and people concerned in that confpiracy. The characters are drawn in lively colours; and there is not a more infamous one amongft them than "*Shanawaz Cawn*," whofe confummate art and addrefs is compared to that of a Bawd, alluding to the circumftance of thofe who follow that profeffion being generally fuch adepts in this fpecies of ability.

This note I have judged requifite to infert entirely in juftice to the Author of the Narrative, as I know there are other writers who make the character in queftion appear. in a very different point of view to that which he does.

7   grounds

grounds of a commencement of hoftilities. A letter from that officer
to Ballajie Row, after his mafter's late
misfortune, was intercepted ; by
which it appeared, that he was fchem-
ing the delivery of Nizam Ally up
to the Mahrattahs. He was confront-
ed with his own letter, but denied the
fact, and infifted that it was a for-
gery by fome of his enemies, to effect
his ruin ; yet, notwithftanding his
perfifting in his innocence, he was
immediately put under clofe confinement. Every thing he had, which
came to a very confiderable amount,
was confifcated, and his dignities and
powers conferred on Monfieur Buffy *,

* A French officer in the fervice of Nizam
Ally and Sallabat Jing. See any of the hiftories
of the war in India.

K 3   who

who now became all in all with Nizam
Ally.

Shanawaz Cawn, in his prifon,
could not forbear plotting his mafter's
deftruction ; but monfieur Buffy,
who had profited fo much by his
fall, was the more immediate object
of his refentment ; and he well
knew that, till Buffy was out of the
way, more extenfive views could not be
accomplifhed. He wrote to Ballajie, ac-
quainting him, that Nizam Ally was
by no means in a ftate to refift him,
being not only in the greateft want
of military ftores, but that, excepting
Monfieur Buffy, he had fcarce an officer of courage or abilities in his
army ; that if Buffy, with his party,
could be but defeated, a victory over
Nizam Ally would quickly fol-

6   low ;

low; which would enfure to him
the entire reduction of the Decan.

This fecond letter fell into Nizam
Ally's hands. Monfieur Buffy was
fent for, and a fhort confultation de-
cided the fate of the traitor, He
was condemned to death; and accordingly fuffered the juft reward of
his perfidy.

Some time after this, Nizam Ally
fent to Ballajie, demanding, that a
fon of Shanawaz Cawn, who, on
his father's confinement, had fled
to that chief, fhould be delivered up.
Ballajie's refufal fo irritated Nizam
Ally, that he gave orders to feize
and imprifon the Mahrattah Vakeel,
then at his court. This drew Ballajie Row's refentment on the diftricts
acknowledging the Mogul govern-

ment;

ment ; and the two armies fpeedi-
ly met once more, to defolate and
lay wafte that unhappy country.

Nizam Ally failed in every attempt, for almoft three months, to
bring the enemy to an engagement ;
in which, moft likely, the advantage of his artillery would have given
him victory : nor had he force fufficient to divide it, and imitate them
in fending detachments to deftroy
fuch parts of their dominions as lay
contiguous to the feat of war.

It was not long till an unavoidable misfortune, increafed by a very
great overfight and bad piece of ge-
neralfhip in Nizam Ally, gave the
Mahrattahs an advantage which did
not efcape the acute obfervation of
their attentive leader.

Both

Both armies were on the banks of
the river Poorna, juſt about the beginning of the rainy feafon; and
the wet rendering Nizam Ally's artillery of little fervice, the attacks of
the Mahrattah cavalry became more
frequent, and likewife more effectual,
than ufual, fo much fo, that Nizam
Ally, after fuſtaining a confiderable
lofs, wifhed to retreat to the oppofite fide of the river; this was ſtre-
nuouſly oppofed by his Dewan, Rajah
Ram Chundar, who juſtly dreaded
the confequence of this meafure, in
front of a fuperior enemy. But, notwithſtanding that officer's remonſtran-
ces, Nizam Ally, at the head of half
his army, croffed the river that day
about noon. Ram Chundar, who
was left with the cannon and remainder

der of the army, was to follow next day. But fuch a quantity of rain fell in the interim, as rendered the river impaffible. The fituation of the Mogul army, and the impracticability of the evil being remedied, was quickly perceived by Ballajie Row, who pointing out the certainty of fuccefs to Ragounath Row, and his other officers, led them to the charge, which was received by the enemy with equal fpirit. But the efforts of valor were rendered ineffectual, from the fuperior number they had to oppofe; and the death of Ram Chundar was foon followed by the entire defeat of his party.

Nizam Ally faw, with an aching heart, the fatal confequence of his error. His officers would have now

per-

perfuaded him to make all the hafte he could to Aurungabad, but he was deaf to their remonftrances, and took a refolution which a few days before would have redounded to his honour, and probably might have been attended with the moft flattering fuccefs ; but which, in his prefent dif-treffed fituation, nothing could juftify, and vexation and defpair in excefs only could have dictated. Reduced and difpirited as his troops were, with them he determined to difpute the paffage of the river, and rifk the event of a battle, but he had foon reafon to repent his obftinacy ; for in a few days, whenever the river was paffable, the Mahrattans croffed it, meeting with but a feeble refiftance, and were completely victorious in the en-

engagement which thereon enfued.
Thus unfortunate, he had little to
expect from the generofity of his enemies. Threats and infulis from Ballajie accompanied the negotiations on
the fubject of a peace, which was
foon after concluded; for the Subah
was in no condition to refufe fuch
terms as were offered to him, however humiliating. The whole Decan
almoft was, on this occafion, given up
to the Mahrattahs; Hyderabad only,
with its dependences, yielding a revenue of about thirty Lack of Rupees
annually, remained in Nizam Ally's
poffeffion.

From that period we find no exertion in the Mogul government to
regain its fuperiority in the fouthern
provinces, nor objecting in other
parts

parts to the regular payment of the
chout, till the wild idea of univerſal
dominion in Hindoſtan was entertained by ſome of Ballajie's coun-
ſellors, and too prematurely adopted
by that chief, whoſe late ſucceſſes,
together with a view of the very de-
bilitated ſtate of the Mogul power
throughout the whole empire, induced him too readily to give his
aſſent to the plan propoſed for de-
throning the Great Mogul, and eſtab-
liſhing the ancient Hindoo government; but the loſs of his eldeſt ſon
Wiſſwaſs Row, and the other fatal con-
ſequences which attended the expedition * fitted out to accompliſh this de-
ſign, operated ſo ſtrongly in his mind,
as to deprive him of reaſon for ſome

* See p. 108, 109.

months

months before his death, which foon after followed.

My only aim in giving this tranf-lation to the public being to convey fome general ideas of a people (at leaft from that period in which they became confiderable as an indepen-dent government), at a time when the prefent tranfactions in India I judged might render it not unaccep-table; I will here drop the narrative, and conclude with a concife ac-count of one family, which, in fu-ture times, may be feen of no lefs importance in the Englifh hiftory with the Mahrattahs than it has al-ready been in their connection and intercourfe with the Mahometan pow-ers.

To

To thofe in the fmalleft degree
converfant in Mahrattah affairs, it
muft appear I mean that family of
Bramins who for feveral generations,
by poffeffing the office of Peifhwa, had
engroffed to themfelves fo very principal a fhare in the government of
that diftinguifhed people. I have already had occafion in the courfe of
this narrative to mention Ballajie
Row and other individuals of this family, and I fhall now proceed to give
a more minute account of it from its
firft elevation to power.

Wiffoojie Punt was a Bramin and
a native of Sewurdun the principal
village of a fmall Purgunnah near the
fea, a few miles diftant from our fet-
tlement of Bancote, or Fort Victoria,
on the coaft of Malabar. He had the
re-

reputation of being well-fkilled in the fciences of aftronomy and aftrology; and many of his predictions having been believed by the people of the country to have been eventually verifi-ed, Jacoot Cawn, Hubfhie Governor of Rajpoorie, on the ftrength of this re-putation, appointed him his fecretary and confident in all matters of con-fequence.

Wiffoojie Punt had one fon, whofe name was Wifshoonaut. When this Wifshoonaut was at an age fit for bufinefs, the Deffai * of Sewerdun hap-pened to die without children, and Wiffoojie had influence enough with the governor of Rajpoorie to get his fon appointed to that office; and

* This, and other offices of government in the Eaft, generally defcends by hereditary right.

when

when his father died, he fucceeded
him alfo as fecretary to Jacoot Cawn
Hubfhie. Thefe two offices he held
till his death.

He left one fon, named Ballajie
Ram, who, from his early years,
fhewed an inclination for the military
life, not much to his father's fatisfaction, who would fain have dif-
fuaded him from it ; but feeing the
ftrong bent of the youth to this profeffion, he at laft confented, and, provided with recommendations from
Jacoot Cawn, Ballajie fet out for Sattarah, where his firft command in
Sewajie's fervice was only a fmall troop
of horfe. In this fituation his activity as an officer, together with his
engaging manners, acquired him the
friendfhip and confidence of all who

L   knew

knew him, and foon raifed him to
higher honours. He particularly attracted the notice and approbation of
Jaderow (then Sewajie's principal officer), who recommended him ftrongly to the Rajah as a young man of
diftinguifhed merit and promifing
abilities. He was hereupon promoted
to the command of a hundred horfe,
with a falary of 5000 rupees a year.
His reputation being thus eftablifhed,
when his father died, Jacoot Cawn
permitted his fucceeding to the office
of Deffai of Sewurdun, and to difcharge the duties of it by deputy.

In Sewajie's wars with Aurungzebe
that Rajah readily difcovered Ballajie
Ram's abilities as an officer; and, from
the favourable opinion he entertained
of him, he gave him the command of

500

500 horfe ; with which Ballajie Ram, by repeated inftances of valour and fidelity, juftified the favours and encouragement which had been fhewn him.

He was ever faithful to Sewajie's caufe, and at laft died of the wounds he received in fupporting it, when Aurungzebe fubdued that Rajah. His death happened before Sewajie was deferted.

Ballajie Ram bore the character of an able ftatefman, as well as a brave warrior. He left two fons, the eldeft named Bajerow, and the other Chimnajie Oppah, who had both accompanied him fome time before his death. Bajerow fucceeded his father in the command and honours in Sewajie's fervice. Chimnajie likewife remain-

ed

ed with him in a more fubordinate
ftation, but aftewards diftinguifhed
himfelf by conquering the fettle-
ments of Salfette and Baffeen *, from
the Portuguefe, about the year 1740.
Both imitated their father in a zea-
lous attachment to Sewajie and his
family; they did not defert him in
the day of adverfity; but, contrary
to the example of thofe by whofe dif-
affection Sewajie's fall was at leaft
haftened, they remained fteady in
their loyalty to him, and were both
taken prifoners when Sewajie, with
his whole family, was reduced to
that fituation. They remained in
captivity only about twelve months,

* Two places of ftrength and importance
near Bombay; and now in the Eaft India Company's poffeffion.

when

when they were releafed, with Tarra-
bai, and the reft of Sewajie's family,
who, as we have feen in the courfe of
the narrative, went to Nagpore. Bajerow attended them thither ; and the
reader has been told likewife how he
was repaid for his faithful adherence
to them, and what change of fortune
he himfelf experienced before his
death.

From a general view of the Mahrattah Hiftory it appears, that fince
Sewajie's time the Rajah of Sattarah,
and acknowledged head of the Mahrattah State, has been nothing more
than a nominal fovereign ; and that
the reins of government have been
held by fome one or other of the
family now in queftion.

L 3　　　　　Ba-

Bajerow had three fons. One of them (the fecond) died when but a young man. The other two are remarkable in hiftory : Ballajie Row for the fucceffes we have feen his military operations attended with : and Ragounath Row, or Ragoubah, (now living) for his misfortunes, and the part he has borne in the prefent Mahrattah war.

Ballajie Row had three fons : Wiffwafs Row, the eldeft, was killed before his father's death, at the famous battle of Pannyput, in the neighbourhood of Dhelli in the year 1761*, when the largeft Mahrattah army that ever took the field fuffered an entire defeat by the collected force of the Mahomedan powers in India. This battle proved

* See page 109.

alfo

alfo fatal to Souddabah, the fon of Chimnajie Oppa, a man of moft diftinguifhed abilities, and who contributed greatly to raife the power of the family. There have not, it is true, been wanting pretenders in India, to perfonate this man *; though, I believe, there is little doubt but that he really fell on the occafion I have mentioned.

Madu Row, the fecond fon of Ballajie Row, fucceeded him as Peifhwa. Ragounath Row, or Ragoubah, uncle to this young man, acted for fome time as his Dewan, but by the inftigation of fome of thofe in power,

---

* One in particular in the year 1776, who had raifed a party to fupport his claims to the government, was betrayed into the hands of the minifterial party at Poonah ; and, after a kind of trial, fuffered death as an impoftor.

who

who had a jealous eye towards Ragounath Row, and faw he was likely
to acquire more power and influence
than they wifhed, prevailed upon
Madu Row to feize and imprifon his
uncle; and, during the period of his
government (near twelve years) Ragoubah feldom enjoyed his liberty.

When Madu Row died, he was fucceeded by his brother, Narran Row,
Ballajie's third fon. The murder of
this unfortunate youth, in 1773,
afforded Ragoubah the pretenfions he
affumes to the government. He was
oppofed however from the ftrong
fufpicion of his nephew's murder *

* The taking the life of a Bramin is one of
the fins for which, according to their religious
tenets, there is no expiation; and it is a pu-
nifhment never inflicted on thofe of that caft,
even in the courfe of juftice.

having

having been committed at his inftigation.

Be this as it may, he wanted abilities to fecure himfelf againft fo ftrong
a party of other chiefs as the idea of
his guilt had raifed. He acted with
fear and timidity ; and a civil war enfued. Two years, I believe, had
fcarce elapfed, before he fuffered an
entire defeat on the plains of Arrafs,
in the province of Guzerat ; and fled
from the field of battle to Baunagur,
a fea-port in the gulf of Cambay ;
where, in the utmoft confufion, he
embarked with little baggage, and a
few attendants, on board fome open
boats, for Surat ; where foon after
he (in the beginning of the year
1775) entered into a treaty with the
Englifh, who were, in confideration
of

of grants and ceffions therein ftipulated, to affift him in fupporting his
difputed right to the Peifhwaſhip of
the Mahrattah empire.

In conclufion to the fhort account
I have thus given of this family, it
may not be improper to obferve, that
the wife of Narran Row was faid to
have been with child at the time of
the affaffination of her hufband, and
that fhe was fhortly after delivered of
a male child. Great doubts are entertained of the reality of this circumftance; but let the cafe be as it
may, the Peifhwaſhip continues to be
adminiftered at Poonah in the name of
this child, by the confederated chiefs *,

who

* This confederacy is known in India by the
appellation of Barrabac, or the twelve brothers,
alluding (as fome fay) to the Mahrattah miniftry

who have ever fince Narran Row's death acted in oppofition to Ragounath Row, and he is ftyled in the public acts of government by the name or title of Row Punt Purdham.

niftry confifting originally of this number when the Peifhwa was not the firft in power, as he is now, in that government ; but I have been like-wife affured, that the prefent adminiftration, on the death of Narran Row, was compofed of the above number of Chiefs.

EXPLANATION of India Words,

As they are to be underſtood in the Narrative.

Buckſhie. Pay-maſter General of the Troops, who bears likewiſe a high military command.

Caſt. A tribe, or ſect.

Chout. Literally a tribute of a fourth part of the revenues.

Coſs. A meaſure, from about one and a half to two and a half miles.

Crore of Rupees. A hundred lack, or a million ſterling.

Deſſai. An office high in the revenue department.

Dewan. Receiver General of the Revenues.

Halcarra. A ſpy, or perſon whoſe profeſſion it is to procure intelligence concerning the enemy.

Hijera. The Mahometan æra.

Jaghire. A grant of an eſtate or territory, generally made over to a perſon in conſequence of ſome ſignal ſervices rendered, or expected to be rendered, to government.

Killidar.

Killidar. The military commanding officer of a fort.

Lack of Rupees. A hundred thousand, or twelve thousand five hundred pounds sterling.

Mujlifs. A court, or council of state

Naib. A Vicegerent.

Oomrahs, or *Ameers.* The nobility of the Mogul empire.

Pattels. The principal tillers or cultivators of land, who are likewise, in a certain degree, farmers.

Peishwa. Now the chief in the Mahrattah government.

Purgunnah. A district.

Rupee. A silver coin, which varies in value in different parts in India, but always betwixt two shillings and half a crown.

Subah. Governor or Viceroy of a Province.

Tank. A lake or pond.

Visier. First minister of state to the great mogul.

Zemindar. Landholders, or Farmers.

P. 154. note. r. *Barrabai.*

F I N I S.

ERRATA.

Page 41. line 3. *read* Cullianie, Bhimrie,

Ib. l. 6. *for* thofe *r.* others

63. l. 19. *r.* Malwa

68. l. 18. *r.* Bajerow.

Ib. Chimnajie Oppa ; *and the fame wherever* Chimnajie *occurs*

P. 69. *in the note, r.* fee p. 147.

P. 87. *note,* l. 14. *r.* fec-ul-derjah

P. 94. l. 17. *r.* for that Ameer

P. 100. l. 16. *r.* the throne

P. 106. l. 11. *r.* had managed

P. 115. *after* Suddabah *add a comma*

For EU product safety concerns, contact us at Calle de José Abascal, 56–1°,
28003 Madrid, Spain or eugpsr@cambridge.org.

www.ingramcontent.com/pod-product-compliance
Ingram Content Group UK Ltd.
Pitfield, Milton Keynes, MK11 3LW, UK
UKHW012342130625
459647UK00009B/462